Our Family Treasures

Favorite Mediterranean & Western Inspired Cuisines!

FATIMA AYACHE -SARHAN   FATAT AYACHE -HAMMOUD

EAMAN AYACHE-OMAR   KEFAH ABDALLAH-AYACHE   NANCY KATRIB-AYACHE

Book design and layout by By Design Desktop Publishing Inc.
Many thanks to Sue Impey for all her help and support in the making of this book.

Printed in Canada

This book was printed by Blitzprint
#1 1235 64 Avenue South East
Calgary, Alberta, Canada, T2H 2J

This book can be ordered from www.familytreasurescookbook.ca

Library and Archives Canada Cataloguing in Publication

Our family treasures : favorite Mediterranean & western inspired cuisines / Fatima Ayache-Sarhan ... [et al.].

Includes index.
ISBN 978-0-9812145-0-4

1. Cookery, Mediterranean. 2. Cookery.
I. Ayache-Sarhan, Fatima

TX714.O872 2009   641.5   C2009-901225-1

Contents

Acknowledgements 8

Appetizers, Dips & Drinks 9

Soups & Salads 29

Meatless 51

Chicken 69

Meats 97

Fish 119

Breads 129

Desserts 159

Index 213

Dedication

To our parents, our in-laws, husbands and our children.

Baalbeck; Lebanon's greatest
Roman treasure. Baalbeck is
a place where visitors can still
recapture the fascination
of the past.

Off the coast of Raouche; this famous natural landmark is known as the Pigeon's Rock of the
Raouche. The two huge rock formations which stand like gigantic sentinels are located in Beirut's
western-most tip and are a popular destination for locals and visitors.

Nestled in the foothills of Canada's Rocky Mountains, Calgary, Alberta is a place where visitors come to explore the heritage of the Canadian West. This safe, clean and vibrant city offers the best of all worlds: a cosmopolitan city of over 1 million people and breathtaking outdoor adventure in pristine wilderness.

Acknowledgements

The five of us got together, sisters and sister-in-laws to create a collection of our most loved recipes. Through each ones life experiences and inspirations we were able to compile this book. Each one of us had their own contributions to Our Family Treasures.

We were all raised in Calgary, Alberta, Canada. Being raised in such a wonderful country we had the opportunity to enjoy our Lebanese heritage and at the same time appreciate our western influences.

Since we were children, the passion to create was in all of us. Our curiosity in the kitchen was what started it all, also the enjoyment of being in the kitchen helped too. The pleasure it gave us when someone was pleased with what they had just eaten was heart felt, especially when they would ask how did you make that? What did you put in it? This inspired us to keep trying new things. To keep creating and experimenting, to find out what was right for us and our families. By sharing each other's experiences, we wanted to create a book in which we could hand down to our children, with hopes that our own children will have experiences and inspirations of their own.

None of this could be possible if it was not for our wonderful families. We must start with our great teachers, our parents, without their guidance none of this would be possible. Their enthusiasm and support is greatly appreciated. Much thanks to our husbands, for their great support and encouragement. We must not forget our children, to whom this book, we hope, will be of great benefit.

These collections of recipes are filled with wonderful memories and experiences. They are a mix of traditional Lebanese, Ethnic, and Modern Day foods. With every recipe there is a story, a gathering of good family times, and memories shared with our loved ones. We hope this cookbook can bring you and your loved ones wonderful moments and everlasting memories.

FATIMA AYACHE-SARHAN

FATAT AYACHE-HAMMOUD

EAMAN AYACHE-OMAR

KEFAH ABDALLAH-AYACHE

NANCY KATRIB-AYACHE

Appetizers, Dips and Drinks

1 Saudi Champagne (page 23)   2 Humous (page 11)

3 Orange Delight (page 25)   4 Spinach Dip (page 19)

Humous - Chickpea Dip

1 can chickpeas with ¼ cup of liquid reserved

3 tbsp Tahini, sesame seed paste

1 small garlic clove

juice of 1 large lemon

¼ cup olive oil

1 tsp salt or to taste

½ tsp black pepper

1½ tsp ground cumin

¼ cup water if needed

In blender add chickpeas and reserved liquid, tahini, garlic, lemon juice, olive oil, salt, pepper and cumin.

Blend for about two minutes or until smooth, if too thick add some water to desired thickness. You can also use a food processor to blend the humous.

Serve with pita bread or use it as a spread in any sandwich.

Fool m'Dammas - Fava Bean Dip

Fatima's special, dedicated to my father-in-law, Assaad Sarhan, who taught me his secret recipes.

2 cans fava beans with ½ cup reserved liquid

1 tsp salt to taste

½ tsp black pepper

1 tsp cumin

juice of 1or 2 lemons or to taste

2 tomatoes, diced small

4 green onions, chopped

¼ cup fresh mint (optional)

½ cup chopped parsley

¼ cup chopped green pepper

½ cup extra virgin olive oil

Pour fava beans and liquid into saucepan. Add salt, pepper, cumin and lemon juice. Stir.

Take a potato masher and slightly mash fava beans. Heat until boiling and take off heat. Place in a serving dish. Stir in tomatoes, onions, mint, parsley, green peppers; pour olive oil on top.

Serve with pita bread for breakfast or brunch.

Baba Ghanouj – Eggplant Dip

2 large eggplants

4 tbsp Tahini (sesame seed paste)

2 cloves garlic, crushed

juice of 2 lemons

1 tsp white vinegar

1 tsp salt or to taste

½ tsp black pepper

¼ tsp cinnamon

¼ cup olive oil

¼ cup parsley, chopped

Wrap eggplants in tin foil until fully covered. Place on cookie sheet and bake in oven at 400°F for about 45 minutes or until tender. Let cool and peel eggplants into a mixing bowl. Add tahini, garlic, lemon juice, vinegar, salt, pepper, and cinnamon.

Take a potato masher and mash up until smooth. If a smoother dip is desired, place mixture into a blender and blend well. Pour into a plate and top with olive oil and parsley. Serve with pita bread.

Taratur – Tahini (Sesame Seed) Sauce

1 cup Tahini (sesame seed paste)

1 cup water

¼ cup parsley chopped

juice of 1 or 2 lemons depending on personal taste

1 clove garlic crushed

1 tsp salt or to taste

½ tsp black pepper

dash of cayenne pepper

Mix tahini with water and blend until smooth. Add in parsley, lemon juice, garlic, salt and peppers. Mix well, blending all the ingredients together. Sauce should be smooth.

This sauce is used for falafel or for fish.

Garlic Sauce

2 garlic cloves

1 egg

1 cup vegetable or canola oil

½ tsp lemon salt

½ to ¾ tsp salt (to taste)

Blend garlic, salt, egg, and lemon salt in food processor or blender. Mix really well.

Then very slowly add oil while the blender is still mixing.

TIP: Use a plastic or glass container that has an adjustable spout, so that when adding oil to blender it becomes easy to add.

Blend until smooth.

Fish Sauce

1 clove garlic
½ bunch parsley
juice of 1 lemon
1 small cucumber
½ cup yogurt
2 tbsp tahini (sesame seed paste)
½ tsp salt or to taste
½ tsp black pepper
½ a jalapeño

Blend all ingredients in a blender until smooth. Serve as a sauce for fish.

Grilled Pita Bread

3 tbsp butter, softened
1 tbsp garlic paste or powder
½ tbsp oregano
½ tbsp basil

Mix all ingredients into bowl, chill in refrigerator for half an hour. Pull apart your favorite pita bread. Spread garlic butter onto both sides.

Fold back over top of each other and cut into four sections to form four triangles.

Open each triangle of pita bread and pull apart so you should have eight separate triangles.

Respread the garlic butter evenly.

Place onto BBQ grill or oven grill, until golden brown.

Cheese Ball

1 package cream cheese
½ cup Monterey Jack cheese, shredded
¼ cup cheddar cheese, shredded
¼ cup chopped cilantro
¼ cup grated onion
1 tbsp chili powder
½ tsp garlic salt
½ tsp dried oregano
¼ tsp dried thyme
¼ tsp dried red pepper flakes
¼ tsp cumin
dash of red pepper sauce
½ cup chopped parsley
assorted crackers

In a bowl beat cream cheese, Monterey Jack, and cheddar cheeses until well blended.

Add in cilantro, onion, chili powder, garlic salt, oregano, thyme, red pepper flakes, cumin, red pepper sauce, and parsley. Mix well blending all the ingredients together.

Shape into a round ball. Cover with plastic wrap and refrigerate for at least two hours.

Serve with crackers or sliced bread.

Layered Dip for Tortillas

3 ripe avocados, peeled and diced

3 tbsp lemon juice

½ tsp garlic salt

½ tsp hot sauce

2 cups sour cream

1 can sliced olives, drained

2 cups chunky salsa

2 tomatoes, chopped

3 green onion, chopped

2 cups shredded cheddar cheese

tortilla chips

Mash avocados, lemon juice, garlic salt, and hot sauce. Pour into a glass clear dish.

Top with sour cream, then layering olives next. Next layer with salsa. Then layer with tomatoes. Top with onions and then with cheese.

Serve with tortilla chips. Enjoy!

Stuffed Mushrooms

5 chicken strips, diced
30 large fresh mushrooms
½ lb ground beef
3 tbsp chopped parsley
$^1/_3$ cup grated Parmesan cheese
1½ cups flavored croutons, crushed
1½ cups mozzarella cheese, shredded
2 tomatoes, diced small
2 tsp dried oregano
½ tsp dried thyme
½ tsp black pepper
½ tsp onion powder
½ tsp garlic powder
¼ tsp salt
dash of cayenne pepper

In a large skillet, cook the chicken strips. Remove and set aside.

Remove the mushroom stems from the caps; set caps aside. Mince the mushroom stems and add to the skillet with drippings; sauté for 3 minutes. Remove from heat and stir in remaining ingredients and chopped chicken strips.

Firmly stuff the filling into the mushroom caps. Place on a greased baking sheet and bake for 15 minutes at 425°F or until mushrooms are tender.

Bruschetta with Feta

12 slices of French bread cut 1-inch thick
½ cup butter, melted
½ cup olive oil
½ cup crumbled Feta cheese
2 garlic cloves, crushed
1 tbsp basil
2 tomatoes, chopped
¼ cup finely chopped onion

In a bowl, mix the butter and oil; brush onto both sides of bread. Place on a baking tray. Bake at 350°F for 10 minutes or until lightly browned.

Combine the feta cheese, garlic, onion, and basil; sprinkle mixture evenly over the bread slices and top with the diced tomato. Bake 10 minutes or until heated through.

Serve warm.

Cheese Twists

1 package frozen puff pastry
½ cup grated Parmesan cheese
¼ cup shredded cheddar cheese
1 tbsp paprika
1 egg slightly beaten

Thaw puff pastry according to package directions. Heat oven to 425°F. Line a baking sheet with wax paper or parchment paper.

Mix the cheeses and paprika together in a small bowl. Roll a sheet of puff pastry into a rectangle on a lightly floured surface. Brush the pastry with the egg. Sprinkle with the cheese mixture. Press the cheese mixture gently into the pastry dough. Turn the pastry dough over and repeat.

Fold pastry lengthwise in half then cut pastry crosswise into ½ inch strips. Unfold each strip and twist holding both ends. Place the twists onto baking sheet. Bake for 10 minutes or until golden brown.

Pastry Bites

4 cups flour

2 cups milk

1 tbsp salt

1 tbsp baking powder

½ cup oil

1 tbsp sugar

1 tbsp yeast

cheese or hotdogs or cooked chicken (your choice)

1 egg

1 tsp lemon juice

Mix all ingredients together *except choice of filling, egg and lemon juice* to form a soft dough. Knead for 5 minutes. Cover and allow dough to rest for 30 minutes.

Oil your hands and cut the dough into small pieces; roll and shape into rounds or shape into triangles or squares. Fill dough pieces with your choice of filling. Pinch the ends of each pastry, closing your choice of stuffing into the dough. Brush each pastry with some beaten egg mixed with the lemon juice. Bake at 400°F for 30 minutes or until golden.

Spinach Dip

1 package frozen chopped spinach (thawed)

¼ cup chopped green onions

½ cup sour cream

½ cup mayonnaise

1 package dried vegetable soup mix

Squeeze excess moisture from spinach until dry. Add in green onions, sour cream, mayonnaise, and soup mix.

Blend very well and refrigerate for at least an hour. Serve with crackers or sliced bread loaf.

Tomato Salsa

6 tomatoes, chopped

½ cup green onions, chopped

½ cup green peppers, chopped

¼ cup cilantro, chopped

4 tbsp lime juice

1 jalapeno chili, chopped fine

3 cloves garlic, crushed

1 tsp salt

½ tsp cumin

½ tsp black pepper

Mix all the ingredients and blend well. Chill until ready to serve.

Quick and Easy Guacamole

3 ripe avocados, mashed

3 tbsp lemon juice

½ cup salsa

½ tsp salt

½ tsp black pepper

¼ tsp garlic powder

2 tbsp olive oil

Mix all the ingredients together and chill until ready to serve. Serve with bread, crackers, or as a spread in a wrap or a sandwich.

Yogurt Dip – (Laban)

4 litres whole milk (homo milk)
1 cup plain yogurt
salt
extra virgin olive oil

Place milk in a large pot over low heat. Heat milk until just ready to boil, making sure that milk does not scorch.

Cool milk until milk is lukewarm. Use 10 second rule to test if milk is lukewarm, place your finger in the milk, if you are able to keep your finger in the milk comfortably for 10 seconds then the milk is at the right temperature.

Add in plain yogurt and stir until blended. Cover tightly with lid and cover with heavy blanket, set aside.

Let sit undisturbed for 6 hours, it should become firm.

Stir firmed yogurt and pour into cheesecloth. Let drain in a strainer, put a bowl underneath. Usually it takes two days to drain most of liquid.

The purpose of this is to let the excess water to drain from the yogurt to become into a thick dip.

Pour the yogurt out of the cheesecloth into a bowl. Stir in salt, adding about two tablespoons, add more if needed. Stir well and place in an airtight container. Drizzle olive oil on top, making sure to cover all the yogurt dip.

Refrigerate immediately.

Cinnamon Sugar Toasted Pecans

6 cups pecan halves
2 egg whites
2 tsp cold water
¾ cup sugar
2 tsp cinnamon
½ tsp salt

Preheat oven to 250°F. Grease a baking sheet and set aside.

Lightly beat the egg whites in a small mixing bowl; add water and beat until frothy but not stiff. Add pecans and mix until coated well.

Combine the sugar, cinnamon and salt. Sprinkle over pecans and toss. Spread mixture on to baking sheet and bake for 1 hour, stirring occasionally. Cool and store in an airtight container.

Caramel Popcorn

14 cups unsalted popped popcorn
2 cups unsalted roasted peanuts or any type of nut (optional)
1½ cups brown sugar
²/₃ cup butter
½ cup light corn syrup
½ tsp salt
½ tsp baking soda

Heat oven to 250°F. Combine popcorn and nuts in a large mixing bowl. Set aside.

In a saucepan add the brown sugar, butter, corn syrup, and salt; cook over medium heat, stirring occasionally, until bubbly around edges. Continue cooking for 5 minutes; remove from heat. Stir in baking soda until foamy. Pour over the popcorn and nuts. Stir until well coated.

Pour and spread mixture into a baking pan. Bake for 1 hour, stirring every 15 minutes. Remove and allow mixture to cool. Store popcorn mix in an airtight container.

Lemonade

4 cups cold water
1 cup fresh lemon juice
½ cup sugar or to taste
mint for garnish

Pour water into pitcher. Add lemon juice, sugar and mint. Mix well by stirring. Refrigerate until ready to serve.

Raspberry Iced Tea

2 cups cold brewed tea
2 cups raspberry juice, chilled
2 cups sparkling water

Mix all ingredients in pitcher. Garnish with raspberries or lemon slices. Serve immediately.

Saudi Champagne

2 - 1 litre containers of apple juice, chilled
2 cans 7-up or sprite pop, chilled
1 bottle Perrier water, chilled
½ cup sliced apples
½ cup sliced and peeled oranges
handful of fresh mint leaves

Mix apple juice, pop, and water together in a pitcher.

In individual glasses, put a couple of apple and orange pieces in them.

Pour beverage mixture into glasses and top with mint. Serve immediately.

Another way of putting this drink together is to add all the ingredients into the pitcher and pour into glasses, making sure to put some fruit in each glass. Enjoy!

Citrus Punch

2 cups cold water

1 can frozen orange juice

1 can frozen grapefruit juice or pineapple juice

1 bottle sparkling water, chilled or 1 bottle gingerale, chilled

Mix all ingredients together in a large pitcher.

Pour into a punch bowl and garnish with orange slices and raspberries.

Ainar

This spicy tea is made for new mothers and their company

water

10 cinnamon sticks or a handful cinnamon bark pieces

1 tsp fresh or dried ginger

2 tbsp Anise seeds

1 tbsp black seed (Habit al Barakee)- Nigella seeds

2 whole nutmegs, crushed into small pieces

6-10 cloves

walnut halves

sugar or honey

In a large teapot, add cinnamon, ginger, anise seeds, black seed, nutmeg, and cloves to boiling water. Boil until desired strength, for at least an hour on a low steady boil.

When serving, strain tea and top with a handful of walnuts.

Add desired amount of sugar or honey.

Fruit Cocktail

1 cup frozen or fresh strawberries
1 banana
¾ - 1 cup apple juice
2-3 cups ice

Blend all ingredients in blender for 5 minutes.

If it doesn't blend well enough to your liking, add more apple juice.

Add more ice if you prefer the cocktail thicker.

Tip
Using frozen fruit makes the drink a little smoother. In this case you wouldn't need as much ice.

Orange Delight

½ can frozen orange juice concentrate
1 cup water
1 cup milk
1 tbsp vanilla
3 tbsp sugar

Place all ingredients into blender.

Blend until frothy and enjoy over crushed ice or ice cubes if desired.

Strawberry Vanilla Smoothie

1 cup vanilla yogurt

1 cup strawberries, fresh or frozen

½ cup milk

1 tsp vanilla extract

½ cup ice cubes (or more if needed)

Combine all ingredients in a blender for about 1-2 minutes until smooth and creamy.

If consistency is not thick enough add more ice cubes.

The Ultimate Smoothie Milk Shake

1 cup milk

3 tbsp sugar

3 tbsp vanilla

2 cups ice cubes

2 scoops vanilla ice cream

1 can orange juice, frozen concentrate

Blend frozen orange juice, sugar, vanilla, and half of the ice in blender.

Add milk, ice cream, and remaining ice into mixture. Blend for 1- 3 minutes or until smooth. Serve in individual glasses.

Arabic Coffee

The aroma of this coffee is superb, especially once made

1 cup water, cold
2 tsp sugar
1 cardamom pod, optional
2 tbsp espresso or Arabic coffee

Place cold water in a small coffee pot or a special coffee pot with a long handle, known as a raqwi. Add in sugar and cardamom pod, making sure to open it up first.

Bring to a boil over medium heat.

Once it starts to boil, remove from heat and add the coffee, stir. Return to heat and lower heat and let boil gently, making sure it does not overflow. Turn heat off and remove from stove.

Spoon off foam and pour into espresso cups. Let the coffee settle and then pour into the cups.

The coffee is made to taste, whether you like it sweet or not too sweet, more sugar can be added or none at all.

Saudi Coffee

2 ½ cups water
2 tbsp partially roasted ground coffee (green in color)
4 to 6 pods of cardamom
2 tsp ground cardamom
pinch of saffron or ½ tsp turmeric

In a saucepan add water and bring to a boil. Add coffee and cardamom pods stirring constantly for 3 to 5 minutes (watch carefully as it has the tendency to overflow).

In a thermos, add the ground cardamom and saffron. Strain the coffee mixture into the thermos. Stir or shake well. Serve in small demitasse cups with dates or chocolate on the side.

Hot Chocolate

So good on a cold winter day!

3 oz unsweetened baking chocolate
1½ cups water
½ cup sugar
4 cups milk

Heat chocolate and water in saucepan over low heat, making sure to stir constantly until melted and smooth.

Stir in sugar. Heat until it boils.

Stir in milk and heat just until hot. Stir until smooth and serve immediately.

Chai

An Indian inspired spicy drink!

2 cups water
2 cinnamon sticks
6 cardamom pods
6 cloves, whole
1-2 black peppercorns
1 cup milk
3 tbsp sugar, more or less to taste
3 tsp black tea, loose leaf

Put water in a saucepan. Add cinnamon sticks, cardamom pods, cloves, and peppercorns.

Bring to a boil. Lower heat and boil for 10 minutes.

Add milk and sugar, and let simmer on low heat for about a minute.

Add in loose tea and turn off heat. Let tea steep for 2 minutes. Strain tea and serve immediately.

Soups and Salads

1 Tabouli (page 43)

2 Chicken Noodle Soup (page 33)

3 Yogurt Cucumber Salad (page 45)

Beef Broth

1 kg beef shanks or soup bones

8 cups cold water

2 celery stalks with leaves, cut up

1 large onion, quartered

3 carrots, cut up

2 tsp salt

1 tsp black pepper

4 whole cloves

2 bay leaves

¼ cup parsley left uncut

In a large pot add all the ingredients and bring to a boil over medium heat.

Once it begins to boil, lower heat and simmer gently.

Skim off any foam from broth. Cover and simmer for 2 hours. Gently strain the broth using a sieve, discard any vegetables and seasonings.

Remove meat from bones and store cooled meat pieces in the refrigerator until use.

Use the broth right away or cool and refrigerate until use.

Chicken Broth

1 whole chicken or cut up

8 cups cold water

2 tsp salt

1 tsp black pepper

2 bay leaves

2 stalks celery, with leaves, cut up

3 carrots, chopped

1 large onion, quartered

¼ cup parsley springs

In a large pot add all the ingredients on medium heat until it comes to a boil.

Skim off any foam and lower heat to low. Gently let simmer on low heat for one hour.

Pour the chicken and vegetables through a sieve and strain. Save broth; discard vegetables and seasonings. Refrigerate chicken when cooled or use right away.

Use broth right away or refrigerate when cooled.

Chicken Noodle Soup

6 cups chicken broth (see previous page)

4 cups water

4 carrots, peeled and diced or sliced

4 celery stalks, diced

1 medium onion, diced small

2 tbsp chicken bouillon (cubes or granules)

salt to taste

1 tsp black pepper

1½ cups uncooked noodles

reserved chicken from chicken broth, chopped

¼ cup chopped parsley

In a large pot add broth and water, bring to a boil over medium heat.

Add in carrots, celery, onion, bouillon, salt, and pepper. Stir gently and let simmer for 15 minutes or until vegetables are tender. Add in noodles, cooked chicken, and parsley.

Let simmer for an extra 5 minutes and turn off heat. Let sit for another 5 minutes.

Serve with bread or crackers.

Vegetable Soup

6 cups prepared Beef Broth (page 31)

1 cup potatoes, cubed

2 cups frozen mixed vegetables (corn, peas)

1 cup carrots, peeled and diced

1 large onion, diced

½ cup celery, diced

4 ripe tomatoes, peeled and diced

2 tbsp tomato paste

salt to taste

½ tsp black pepper

½ tsp thyme

½ tsp basil

dash of cinnamon

¼ cup chopped parsley

½ cup orzo (optional)

In a large pot add beef broth and bring to a boil over medium heat. Add the rest of the ingredients and gently boil. Boil until all the vegetables are tender, stirring occasionally.

If adding orzo, add it to the soup in the last 5 to 10 minutes of cooking, cook until orzo is tender.

Beef Noodle Stew

So good on a cold day

1lb beef boneless sirloin steak

1 tbsp olive oil

1 onion, large

1 clove garlic, crushed

2 potatoes, diced

200 grams spaghetti or noodles

6 cups water

1 can tomato paste

1 tsp seasoning salt

½ tsp pepper

1 tsp salt

Cut meat into small chunks. Chop onion into small pieces.

Heat oil in a large pot; add onions and crushed garlic. Sauté until browned. Add in meat. Cook on medium heat until meat is cooked. Add potatoes to meat mixture.

Then add spaghetti, cutting them in half. Add water, tomato paste, salts and pepper, stirring well. Boil on medium heat until potatoes and spaghetti are cooked.

Cream of Broccoli Soup

1 kg broccoli, chopped
3 cups water
1 cup celery, chopped
1 large onion, chopped
¼ cup olive oil
2 tbsp butter
2 tbsp flour
3 cups chicken broth (page 32)
salt to taste
1 tsp black pepper
¼ tsp ground nutmeg
½ cup heavy cream

In a stockpot, add broccoli, water, celery and onion. Cook for 10 minutes or until tender. Do not drain. Blend with a hand blender or in a blender until smooth. Set aside.

In a large saucepan, add olive oil and butter; heat until melted. Add flour and mix constantly until smooth and bubbly. Add chicken broth and bring to a boil. Stir in broccoli mixture, salt, pepper and nutmeg. Heat to boiling; remove from heat and add heavy cream.

Minestrone Soup

1 large onion, chopped

2 cloves garlic, minced

¼ cup olive oil

1 - 28 oz can diced tomatoes, do not drain

1 - 14 oz can red kidney beans

4 to 6 cups water

2 celery stalks, chopped

1 cup zucchini, chopped

1½ cups mixed vegetables (corn, and peas)

3 packets beef or vegetable bouillon

½ cup tomato sauce

2 tsp salt or to taste

1 tsp black pepper

1 tsp basil

½ tsp thyme or oregano

¼ cup chopped parsley

½ cup uncooked small pasta (any variety)

In a large pot heat olive oil and add onion and garlic, cook until lightly brown.

Add the rest of the ingredients. Boil over medium heat uncovered for 20 minutes.

Stirring occasionally. Cover and turn off heat. Serve hot.

Lentil (Addas) Soup

This is one of our favourites

1¼ cups yellow or red split lentils

½ cup parboiled rice

1 large carrot, shredded

1 large potato, shredded

½ cup corn, frozen

¼ cup parsley, finely chopped

4 sachets chicken bouillon or 2 chicken bouillon cubes

½ tsp cumin

1 tsp salt or to taste

1 onion, chopped

4 tbsp olive oil

7 cups water

3 cups water

Place lentils in a large pot and add 7 cups of water. Bring to a boil and skim off foam. Boil on medium-low heat until lentils are tender.

In large bowl place the cooked lentils with its water and blend with hand blender until the mixture is smooth.

In a small skillet sauté onions with olive oil until golden brown, set aside.

Place lentil mixture back into large pot and add 3 cups of water and bring to a boil on low heat.

Add rice and cook for about 5 minutes. Add carrots, potatoes, corn, sautéed onions, parsley, chicken bouillon, cumin, and salt. Boil for another 7 minutes or until rice is cooked.

Lentil Soup with Beef

½ cup ground beef

1 onion, grated or chopped

3 tbsp olive oil

1½ cups lentils

10 cups water

1 tsp salt, or to taste

¼ tsp pepper

½ lemon, squeezed

In large pot, sauté meat, onion and olive oil; once meat has browned add lentils and water. Bring to a boil.

Add salt and pepper. Cover and cook until lentils are tender. Add in lemon juice, stir.

Add more lemon juice if desired.

Lentil Soup with Lemon

2 cups brown lentils, washed and drained

6 cups water

3 potatoes, peeled and diced

2 cups Swiss chard, washed and roughly chopped

½ cup olive oil

1 onion, finely chopped

2 tbsp butter

3 to 4 cloves garlic, crushed

½ cup fresh coriander, finely chopped

2 tsp cumin

1 tsp salt or to taste

1 tsp black pepper

dash of cinnamon

½ cup lemon juice or to taste

In a stockpot, place washed lentils and water over medium high heat; bring to a boil. Lower heat and simmer for 25 minutes or until tender; add potatoes and simmer for 15 minutes. If you desire a thicker or thinner soup, adjust the amount of water.

Stir in Swiss chard and lower heat.

In a frying pan, add oil and onions, frequently stir until golden brown.

Add butter, garlic and coriander stir for 1 minute; add mixture to lentils, stir; add cumin, salt, black pepper, cinnamon and lemon juice. Let boil for 2 minutes more and turn off heat.

French Onion Soup

8 cups thinly sliced onion

½ cup olive oil

1 tbsp sugar

2 tsp salt or to taste

1 tsp black pepper

2 tbsp butter

1 tbsp Worchestershire sauce

8 cups beef broth

10 slices French bread, toasted

½ cup Parmesan cheese

1 cup mozzarella cheese

In a large pot, add onions, olive oil, sugar and black pepper; cook over medium heat, stirring frequently until onions are caramelized (brown). Add the beef broth, Worchestershire sauce, salt and butter. Bring to a boil and simmer for 30 minutes.

Place soup in individual oven proof soup bowls. Place one slice of French bread on top of each bowl. Sprinkle with cheeses; broil in oven until cheese is melted. Serve immediately.

Kishk Soup

A powdered soup base made from fermented yogurt and burghul.

1 medium onion, minced
2 or 3 cloves garlic minced
¼ cup olive oil
2 potatoes, peeled and diced
2 cups water
2 tbsp chicken bouillon
1 cup Kishk
3 cups cold water
salt to taste
1 tsp black pepper

In a large saucepan, add onion and olive oil cook until slightly brown; add the garlic and potatoes; stir. Add the 2 cups of water and chicken bouillon. Cook until potatoes are tender. Add the Kishk and cold water (add the cold water a cup at a time until desired consistency is formed, you may need less or more water depending on the desired thickness of soup); season with salt and black pepper. Simmer for 5-10 minutes, stirring frequently until mixture thickens. It will resemble a thick chowder.

Tip
Kishk can be found in most Middle Eastern grocery stores.

Tabouli

5 bunches fresh parsley, chopped fine by hand

½ cup fresh mint, chopped fine

1 bunch green onion, chopped fine

3 large tomatoes, diced very fine

1 large English cucumber, diced very fine (optional)

1 bunch radishes, diced very fine (optional)

½ cup fine crushed wheat (burghul)

1 cup water, cold

2 lemons, large squeezed or to taste

2 tsp salt or to taste

½ cup olive oil, extra virgin

2 leaves of Romaine lettuce, chopped fine (optional)

In a large bowl add parsley, mint, onions, tomatoes and, if desired, cucumbers, radishes and chopped lettuce. In a small bowl add crushed wheat with cold water and let sit for 5 minutes. Drain all the water and add crushed wheat to the salad mixture. Add in lemon juice, salt and olive oil. Mix well altogether and refrigerate until ready to serve. Best if served right away.

Greek Salad

Bring a bit of Greece to your table!

10 romaine lettuce leaves

1 cucumber

2 tomatoes

1 red onion

1 green pepper

12 black olives

¼ cup feta cheese (crumbled)

1 tbsp dried oregano

¼ cup olive oil

2 tbsp lemon juice

Wash lettuce, cucumber, tomatoes, red onion, and green pepper.

In a bowl, chop vegetables into bite sized pieces. Add olives, feta cheese, dried oregano, olive oil and lemon juice. Mix well and refrigerate until ready to serve.

Macaroni Salad

1 cup macaroni pasta (uncooked)

4 cups water

½ cup broccoli, chopped

10 cherry tomatoes, cut in halves

1 carrot, peeled and shredded

2 tbsp green relish

¾ cup mayonnaise

¼ cup milk

½ tsp salt

½ tsp pepper

In a large pot bring water to a boil, add macaroni. Let cook on medium heat for approximately 7 minutes.

Then add chopped broccoli to the macaroni. Let boil for an extra 2 minutes, making sure not to overcook. Drain and rinse with cold water.

Pour pasta and broccoli in large bowl. Add halved tomatoes and grated carrots to bowl. In another bowl add relish, mayonnaise, milk, salt and pepper. Mix until smooth. Add the mayonnaise mixture to the pasta and vegetables. Mix well. Refrigerate for at least 2 hours.

Enjoy!

No Mayo Coleslaw

½ head cabbage, sliced thin

4 carrots, peeled and shredded

½ cup vegetable or canola oil

2 tbsp sugar

1 tsp salt

1 tbsp vinegar

½ tsp garlic powder

Mix the cabbage and carrots together in a large mixing bowl; set aside. In a small bowl add the oil, sugar, garlic powder, salt and vinegar; mix well. Pour over cabbage mixture and mix well. Refrigerate for at least 30 minutes.

Yogurt Cucumber Salad

Perfect on a hot summer's day!

1 garlic clove

1½ tbsp salt

2 cups plain yogurt

¼ cup water

1 English cucumber

1 tbsp dried mint

Crush garlic with salt in large bowl. Add yogurt and stir. Then add water to yogurt mixture and stir gently.

Chop cucumber into small pieces. Add cucumbers and mint to the yogurt mixture, stirring well. Refrigerate for at least 1 hour.

Delicious with lentils and rice and with chicken kabobs.

Potato Salad

4 large potatoes, peeled

6 cups water

1 cup celery, chopped

¼ cup onion, minced (optional)

1 tbsp vinegar

1 tbsp mustard

¾ cup mayonnaise

¼ cup milk

1 tsp salt

¼ tsp pepper

Cut peeled potatoes into thick slices. Boil water in a large pot. Once water boils add the potatoes. Let boil until tender. Drain and cool. Once cooled, chop and dice potatoes in a large bowl.

Add chopped celery and minced onion. In another bowl add mayonnaise, milk, salt, pepper, vinegar and mustard. Blend well. Pour on top of potato mixture and mix well. Refrigerate until ready to serve.

Potato and Egg Salad

4 potatoes (medium sized)

4 cups water

4 eggs

4 cups water

¼ tsp pepper

½ tsp salt

3 tbsp olive oil

1 lemon, squeezed

3 tbsp white vinegar

½ cup mayonnaise

Put water into two large pots. Bring both pots of water to a boil. Wash potatoes with peel left on and add to one of the pots. Boil until potatoes are tender. Drain water and add cold water to the pot. Peel potatoes and chop into cubes. Place cubed potatoes in a large bowl and set aside.

Gently add the eggs to the second pot and let boil for approximately 8 minutes. Drain water and add cold water to the eggs, this stops the cooking process. Peel the eggs and chop into cubes. Add to the potatoes. Add pepper, salt, oil, lemon juice, vinegar and mayonnaise. Mix well. Refrigerate until ready to serve.

Egg Salad

4 eggs

4 cups water

pinch of salt, or to taste

½ tsp black pepper

½ cup mayonnaise

1 tbsp mustard (optional)

½ cup celery, chopped (optional)

bread

Put water in a large pot. Bring water to a boil. Gently add the eggs. Let boil for approximately 8 minutes. Drain water and add cold water to the eggs, this stops the cooking process.

Peel the eggs. Using a potato masher, mash the eggs in a bowl. Add mayonnaise, mustard, chopped celery, salt and black pepper. Mix well. Refrigerate until ready for use.

To make sandwiches with this salad, simply spread a couple of tablespoons between 2 slices of bread, serve.

Fattoush

1 head romaine lettuce

3 green onions, chopped

5 radishes, thinly sliced

2 large tomatoes, chopped

1 bunch parsley, finely chopped

1 long English cucumber, sliced

1 green pepper, diced

1 yellow pepper, diced

1 red pepper, diced

½ bunch fresh mint, chopped or 2 tbsp dried mint

3 tbsp zaatar (or dry oregano leaves)

¼ cup lemon juice

1 tbsp salt

¼ cup olive oil

3 tbsp canola oil

3 tbsp sumac

1 large pita bread fried or toasted in oven, broken into bite size pieces

Wash and drain lettuce. Chop into bite sized pieces and place into large bowl. Add remaining chopped vegetables, and toss well.

Add mint, zaatar, lemon juice, salt, oils and sumac. Add broken pita bread pieces and serve immediately.

Tip
To add more flavor to your salad, toast 2 large pita breads in oven until crisp. Break into small pieces and place into a bowl. Sprinkle with 2 tbsp zaatar (oregano mix), 1 tbsp sumac, 1 tsp lemon salt, ½ cup olive oil. Mix until well coated. Add preferred amount to your salad.
Store in an airtight container.

Caesar Salad

1 head romaine lettuce
1 cup croutons
½ cup Caesar dressing
2 tbsp freshly grated Parmesan cheese

Wash and drain lettuce. Chop into bite sized pieces and put into a large bowl.

Add croutons and Parmesan cheese. Then add the Caesar dressing and toss until mixed really well. Serve and eat immediately.

Garden Salad

1 head romaine lettuce
2 tomatoes
1 English cucumber
1 carrot, grated
½ cup red cabbage, grated
1 cup celery, chopped

Wash and drain lettuce. Chop lettuce, tomatoes, and cucumber into bite sized pieces and put into a large bowl.

Add grated carrots and cabbage and chopped celery. Top with your favourite dressing and toss. Serve immediately and enjoy!

Lebanese Salad

1 head romaine lettuce

2 tomatoes

1 English cucumber

3 radishes, thinly sliced

1 green onion

1 lemon, freshly squeezed

⅓ cup olive oil

⅛ tsp pepper

1½ tsp salt or to taste

1 tsp dry oregano leaves

½ bunch fresh mint or 2 tbsp dry mint

Wash and drain lettuce. Chop lettuce, tomatoes and cucumbers into bite sized pieces and put into a large bowl. Add in radishes.

Chop green onions into small pieces and add to bowl. Next, add the lemon juice and oil. Add salt, pepper, oregano leaves, and mint. Mix well. Serve immediately.

Taco Salad

1 - 250 g pkg regular or light cream cheese (at room temperature)

½ cup regular or light sour cream

1 cup salsa (hot, medium or mild)

1 cup medium cheese salsa

½ green or red pepper (optional)

1 tomato, cubed

½ cup lettuce, shredded

½ cup cheddar cheese, grated

Mix cream cheese and sour cream really well with hand mixer. Spread cream cheese and sour cream mixture in a glass bowl (preferably clear to see all the different layers).

Pour cheese salsa on top of the cream cheese and sour cream mixture and then spread out the salsa on top of that.

Layer the tomatoes, peppers, and lettuce. Top with the grated cheese and chill for 30 minutes. When ready to eat, serve with tortilla chips and enjoy.

Tomato and Cucumber Salad

5 tomatoes, cubed

1 long English cucumber, cubed

1 onion, chopped (optional)

1 clove garlic, crushed

1 tbsp dried or freshly chopped mint

1 tsp salt, or to taste

¼ tsp pepper

¼ cup olive oil

juice of ½ lemon, or to taste

¼ tsp sumac (optional)

Put tomatoes, cucumbers and onion in a large bowl. Add remaining ingredients and mix well.

Serve with burghul pilaf.

Meatless Dishes

Fetti –
Pita bread and chick peas

Nancy's Special, dedicated to my grandmother, Zeinab Berjawi, who I love very dearly and is always there to inspire me.

1½ pita bread, large (toasted until golden brown)

1 cup yogurt, plain

¼ cup tahini, sesame paste

1 garlic clove, crushed

1 can chick peas 19 oz + ½ liquid of can

½ tsp salt

1 tbsp butter

¼ cup pine nuts, toasted, or almonds, toasted

½ cup ground beef, cooked (optional)

Piece up toasted pita bread into bite sized pieces, place in the bottom of casserole dish. Combine plain yogurt, tahini and crushed garlic in a bowl, mix well and set aside.

In a saucepan heat up the chickpeas, including half of the liquid. Add salt then bring to a boil for approximately 2 minutes.

Pour hot chickpeas and liquid on top of pita bread pieces.

Then pour the yogurt mixture over the chickpeas.

In a saucepan, melt butter and pour over dish. Top with pine nuts or almonds and meat if desired.

This dish is to be eaten right away. Enjoy!

Burghul Pilaf

2 tbsp olive oil
1 cup coarse crushed wheat (burghul or bulgar)
¾ tsp salt, or to taste
¼ tsp pepper
2 cups water

Heat oil in large pot. Add in coarse crushed wheat and stir.

Add water, bring to a boil and then add salt, and pepper.

Cover and cook on low heat for about 20 minutes.

Serve with salad.

Rice Pilaf

1 tbsp butter
¼ cup vermicelli
1 cup rice, rinsed
2 cups water
½ tsp salt

In medium pot, melt butter and lightly brown vermicelli. Add rice and stir.

Add water and salt.

Bring to a boil. Cover and cook on low heat for 20 minutes or until rice is fully cooked and all the water has evaporated.

Rice with an Egyptian Flare

This rice may be served with fish, chicken or meat dishes.

4 cups cold water

1 cup shredded carrots

3 pods cardamom

1-2 cinnamon sticks

½ tsp allspice

1 tsp cumin seeds

1 large onion, sliced thin

¼ cup olive oil

salt to taste

2 cups rice (preferably Basmati rice)

In a large stock pot, add all the ingredients except rice. Bring to a boil on high heat, lower heat and boil for 6 minutes. Add washed rice and stir; cover and lower heat. Simmer for 15 to 20 minutes or until water has evaporated and rice is tender.

Nut and Raisin Topping

2 tbsp butter

¼ cup pine nuts or slivered almonds

¼ cup golden raisins

Fry nuts in butter until golden brown then mix in the golden raisins; sprinkle on top of rice after it is cooked and plated.

Dilled Rice with Mixed Vegetables

2 cups washed and rinsed basmati rice (use cold water)

½ tsp black pepper

1 tsp salt

1 tsp vegetable seasoning (optional)

¼ cup chopped dill

1 cup frozen mixed vegetables

2 tbsp butter

4 cups cold water

or

2 cups cold water and 2 cups chicken stock

Add all ingredients in rice cooker and follow manufacturer's directions or if you are using your stove top, place all ingredients in a large pot. Bring to a boil, reduce heat and simmer for 20 minutes or until water has evaporated and rice is tender.

Stuffed Grape Leaves – Warak Inaab

1 jar grape leaves
2 cups rice, calrose style
1 bunch parsley, finely chopped
2 tbsp dried mint
2 tomatoes, finely diced
¼ cup olive oil
1 tbsp lemon salt
1 tbsp salt
1 tbsp pepper
juice of 1 lemon
water

Drain grape leaves and place in a large bowl filled with warm water to wash off the brine.

Wash well and drain all the water.

In another bowl wash rice well and drain. Mix in parsley, mint, tomatoes, olive oil, lemon salt, salt, pepper, and juice of one lemon. Mix well.

Take one grape leaf and place on a cutting board shiny side down and the stem part facing you. If there is a stem on the leaf cut it off with a sharp knife.

Place a teaspoon of rice mixture in a thin row across the leaf. Take sides of leaf and fold over into the middle, then take the bottom and roll up tightly making sure the edges stay in the middle and rolling it up like a jelly roll. Repeat for all the grape leaves. Layer in a large pot. Place grape leaves next to each other (going in one direction). When starting the next layer, place grape leaves going in the opposite direction of the first layer – it will have a crisscross effect.

Keep alternating until all have been layered. Place a round oven safe glass dish on the top of the grape leaves. This helps keep the stuffed leaves in their place. Add enough water to cover the top of the plate and all the stuffed leaves are submerged.

Cook on low heat for about an hour and a half to two hours or until rice has cooked. Drain any excess water.

When the grape leaves have cooked let cool down and place on a serving platter and enjoy.

Lentils and Rice – Majadarra

1 cup lentils

8 cups water

¾ cup rice

1 tsp salt

¼ tsp pepper

¼ tsp cayenne pepper

½ tsp cumin

1 onion, chopped

¼ cup olive oil

In a large pot bring water to a boil and add lentils. Cover and let boil for 45 minutes or until tender over medium-low heat.

Rinse rice in a bowl and add to lentils. If more water is needed add more to the lentil mixture.

Add salt, peppers and cumin. Lower heat to a medium boil.

Cover and cook for about 20 minutes or until almost all the water has evaporated.

Meanwhile, in a frying pan cook onions with oil until onions are golden brown over low heat.

Add to cooking lentils, stirring once. Remove from heat when all the water has evaporated and rice has cooked.

Serve with pickles, pickled cabbage, hot peppers, Lebanese salad, or Plain yogurt.

Lentils and Burghul

1 cup lentils
8 cups water
¾ cup coarse crushed wheat (burghul or bulgar)
1 tsp salt
¼ tsp pepper
¼ tsp cayenne pepper
½ tsp cumin
1 onion, chopped
¼ cup olive oil

In a large pot bring water to a boil and add lentils. Cover and let boil for 45 minutes or until tender over medium-low heat.

Rinse crushed wheat and add to lentils. Add salt, peppers and cumin. Let boil over medium-low heat. If more water is needed add more.

In a frying pan cook chopped onions with oil until lightly golden over low heat.

Add onion mixture to the lentil mixture, just stirring once. Remove from heat when all the water has evaporated and the crushed wheat has cooked.

Serve with pickles, Lebanese salad, or plain yogurt.

Burghul and Chickpeas

¼ cup olive oil

1 onion, finely chopped

1 cup coarse crushed wheat (burghul or bulgar)

1 can chickpeas, 19 oz

3 cups water

2 tbsp tomato paste

1 tsp salt

¼ tsp pepper

¼ tsp cayenne pepper

¼ tsp cumin

¼ tsp garlic salt

¼ tsp seasoning salt

In a large pot add oil and onion. Cook over low heat until onion is tender and lightly browned. Add crushed wheat and chickpeas. Stir.

Add water, tomato paste and seasonings. Stir and let boil over low heat until all the water is absorbed. Serve with pickles.

Burghul and Tomatoes

¼ cup olive oil

1 onion, finely chopped

3 tomatoes, ripe diced

1 cup coarse crushed wheat (burghul or bulgar)

2 tbsp tomato paste

3 cups water

1 tsp salt

¼ tsp pepper

¼ tsp cumin

¼ tsp garlic salt

¼ tsp seasoning salt

In a large pot add oil and onion. Cook over low heat until onion is tender. Add in diced tomatoes. Cook tomatoes for five minutes stirring occasionally.

Add in crushed wheat, tomato paste, water and seasonings. Stir.

Cook over low-medium heat until all the water is absorbed. Serve with pickles.

Burghul Balls with Yogurt – Dahareej and Laban

1 cup fine crushed wheat (burghul or bulgar)

1½ cups water, warm

½ cup flour

1 tsp salt

½ tsp cumin

¼ tsp pepper

8 cups water

6 cups yogurt, plain

½ cup water, cold

1 clove garlic, crushed

1 tsp salt

1 tsp dried mint

In a large bowl add crushed wheat and warm water. Soak for 5 minutes. Drain, leaving only a little bit of water.

Add flour, salt, cumin, and pepper. Mix well. Mixture should be a little sticky. Add more warm water or flour if needed.

Shape into small round marble sized balls. Place on a clean tray.

Pour water in a large pot. Bring to a boil over medium heat.

Gently drop balls into boiling water. Put only half of mixture in the water at a time.

Let the balls cook for 20 minutes or until tender. Drain and set aside until all the burghul balls have cooked.

In a large bowl, add yogurt, water, garlic, salt, and dried mint. Mix well.

When the burghul balls have cooled, gently add them to the yogurt mixture.

Refrigerate until ready to be served.

Potato Casserole

3 medium potatoes, diced large
2 medium zucchini, diced large
2 medium carrots, diced large
2 cloves garlic, crushed
1 - 19 oz can tomato sauce
1 tsp seasoning salt
½ tsp pepper
¼ tsp cinnamon
1 tbsp parsley

Preheat oven to 375ºF

In a large casserole dish, place diced potatoes, zucchini, and carrots.

In a bowl combine garlic, tomato sauce, salt, pepper, cinnamon, and parsley.

Pour sauce over vegetables.

Bake in oven for 30-40 minutes or until vegetables are tender.

Mashed Potatoes

10 cups water
1 tsp salt
6 large potatoes, peeled and sliced
2 tbsp butter
¼ cup milk
2 tbsp salt

In a large pot pour water and 1 teaspoon of salt and bring to a boil.

Add in potatoes. Let boil on medium heat until the potatoes are tender.

Drain potatoes. Transfer potatoes into a large bowl.

Take a potato masher and mash the potatoes. Add in butter continuing to mash.

Add in the milk and salt, adding more if needed. The potatoes should be creamy and smooth.

Spinach and Rice

1 onion, finely chopped

¼ cup olive oil

1 spinach, bunch

1 cup rice

2 ½ cups water

1 tsp salt

¼ tsp pepper

¼ tsp cayenne pepper

¼ tsp garlic salt

½ tsp chicken bouillon

In a large pot add oil and onion. Cook on low heat until onion is tender.

Wash spinach and chop into bite sized pieces. Add to pot. Cook for five minutes on low heat, stirring occasionally.

Add washed rice, water, and seasonings. Stir once and let cook on low heat until all the water is absorbed and rice is tender.

Zucchini and Tomatoes

1 tbsp olive oil

1 onion, diced

3 garlic cloves, minced

4 zucchini, diced

1 - 14 oz can chopped or diced tomatoes

1 tsp cumin

½ tsp black pepper

1 tsp salt or to taste

¼ tsp cinnamon

In a large pot add oil, onion, and garlic. Cook over medium heat until onions are slightly golden in colour. Add in zucchini and cook for a minute. Add in tomatoes and seasonings. Stir and let cook for 15 minutes or until the zucchini is tender.

Can be eaten with pita bread.

Zucchini and Eggs

1 tbsp olive oil

1 onion, chopped

3 garlic cloves, minced

4 zucchini, diced

6 eggs, slightly beaten

1 tsp cumin

½ tsp black pepper

1 tsp salt or to taste

½ tsp seasoning salt

In a large pot add oil, onion and garlic. Cook over medium heat until onions are slightly golden in colour. Add in zucchini and cook until tender and until there is no liquid from the zucchini left.

Add in eggs and seasonings. Mix gently and cook until all the eggs are cooked.

Serve with pita bread.

> Tip
>
> You can use the scooped out flesh from hollowed out zucchinis from the stuffed zucchini recipe to make these recipes.

Tortellini Alfredo

1 pkg tortellini
2 tbsp flour
2 tbsp butter or margarine
1¼ cups heavy cream
1 tsp garlic powder
¼ tsp salt
¼ tsp oregano
¼ tsp basil
¼ tsp pepper
1¼ cups Parmesan cheese, grated

Cook tortellini according to package directions.

Mix flour and butter in saucepan until butter is melted. Mix in heavy cream gradually until it forms a smooth texture. Add remaining ingredients; stir until sauce is blended.

Boil for 3 5 minutes at low heat. Remove from heat. Add to drained tortellini and toss until pasta is well coated.

Vegetable Tortellini

1 pkg fresh tortellini (cheese filled)

8 cups water

1 tbsp olive oil

1 clove garlic, crushed

2 cans cream of mushroom soup

¼ cup Parmesan cheese

½ cup milk

2 cups water

½ cup cauliflower, chopped

½ cup carrots, sliced

½ cup broccoli, chopped

In a large pot bring first amount of water to a boil. Add pasta and cook pasta as directed on package, drain and set aside.

Heat olive oil in a large pot. Add garlic, soup, cheese, and milk. Stir until blended.

Bring to a boil, set aside.

In a small pot boil the second amount of water. Add carrots and cauliflower. Boil for 3 minutes then add the broccoli, let boil for another 2 minutes, then drain.

Add vegetables to the sauce mixture and then add cooked tortellini and gently stir together. Let heat through until bubbly.

Serve immediately.

Spinach Tortellini

1 pkg fresh tortellini (cheese filled)
8 cups water
1 tbsp salt
2 tbsp butter
2 tbsp flour
1 clove garlic, grated finely
¾ cup milk
1 tsp salt
¼ tsp pepper
1 pkg frozen chopped spinach, thawed
1 can artichoke hearts, drained and pieced
½ cup cheddar cheese, grated

In a large pot add water and first amount of salt, bring to a boil. Add in tortellini and boil gently for 5 minutes. Drain and set aside.

In another pot melt butter over medium heat. Add in flour and grated garlic, mixing together.

Gently pour in milk and stir well. Let simmer on low heat. Add more milk if needed.

Add in salt, pepper, spinach, and artichoke pieces. Mix well.

Add the tortellini to the sauce mixture. Set aside.

Pour into a greased casserole dish and top with cheese. Cover with foil.

Bake in a 350°F oven for 30 minutes. Serve with garlic bread.

Chicken

Fried-Oven Chicken

Crispy and delicious!

¼ cup butter
½ cup flour
½ tsp paprika
½ tsp salt
¼ tsp pepper
1 chicken, whole cut up

Heat oven to 400°F. Melt butter in saucepan. Pour into large bowl and cool.

Mix in flour, paprika, salt and pepper.

Coat chicken pieces with the flour mixture.

Place chicken pieces into a large baking pan and bake uncovered for 30 to 40 minutes or until no longer pink when thickest pieces are pierced.

Barbequed Chicken

So simple to make and so tasty!

2 lbs chicken legs with backs attached
¼ cup vinegar
¼ cup lemon juice
¼ cup oregano, dried
¼ cup canola oil
1 tbsp seasoning salt

In a large bowl mix all the ingredients and make sure to coat the chicken well.

Preheat barbeque and cook the chicken legs until fully cooked. Make sure to flip at least once and pierce chicken to make sure it is cooked and no longer pink inside.

Baked Stuffed Chicken

The stuffing is the best part!

1 whole roasting chicken

1 cup rice

½ cup ground beef, cooked

¼ cup pine nuts or slivered almonds, toasted

1 tsp salt

2 tsp cinnamon

½ tsp black pepper

1 tsp seasoning salt

2 tbsp olive oil

Heat oven to 375°F.

Wash chicken and place on cutting board. Take large pot and boil rice for 10 minutes. Drain and cool rice. In a large bowl add rice, cooked ground beef and toasted nuts (to toast nuts place a tablespoon of butter in a skillet and add the nuts on low heat stirring often). Add salt, cinnamon, black pepper, seasoning salt and olive oil. Mix well.

Fill the cavity of the chicken and also under the chicken's skin with the stuffing mixture. Place chicken in a roasting pan breast side up. Drizzle olive oil over the chicken and sprinkle with salt and pepper. Bake covered for 1 hour, then uncover and let cook for another half hour or until meat thermometer reads 180°F and juice is no longer pink when center of thigh is cut. Let stand for 20 minutes for easier carving.

(See picture at beginning of the chapter)

Baked Chicken and Vegetables

This is as easy as it gets!

1 whole roasted chicken, cut up

4 potatoes, large

4 carrots, large

2 onions

1 tsp salt

½ tsp pepper

1 tsp seasoning salt

2 tbsp olive oil

Preheat oven to 375°F.

Wash chicken pieces and place in a large roasting pan. In a large bowl peel and wash potatoes, carrots and onions. Cut vegetables in halves. Arrange vegetables around chicken pieces. Drizzle olive oil on chicken and vegetables. Top with salt, pepper and seasoning salt. Bake covered for 1 hour, then uncover and cook for 15 more minutes until chicken is golden and meat thermometer reads 180°F. Serve warm and if desired serve with gravy.

Seasoned Chicken Breasts

Oh so simple and versatile!

4 chicken breasts, boneless
2 tbsp olive oil
1 tbsp Montreal steak spice
½ tsp salt
½ tsp pepper
¼ tsp cinnamon
3 bay leaves
1 tbsp oregano

Preheat oven to 375°F.

Arrange chicken breasts in a 13 by 9 inch roasting pan. Drizzle olive oil over the chicken. Sprinkle seasonings on chicken. Put bay leaves in pan. Cover with tin foil and bake for about 45 to 60 minutes; turning the chicken once half way through.

Slice cooked chicken breasts and make into sandwiches in pita bread with garlic sauce, lettuce, pickles, tomatoes, pickled cabbage, hot sauce or hot peppers. Toast if desired.

Potato Stuffed Chicken

What a real treat and so satisfying!

4 chicken breasts, boneless

½ tsp salt

½ tsp pepper

½ tsp Montreal steak spice

½ tsp Italian spice mix

½ tsp garlic powder

4 portions mashed potatoes, previously made

½ cup cheddar cheese, grated

Preheat oven to 375°F.

With thick side of chicken breast facing up, make an incision to each chicken breast but not fully to the end, making a butterfly effect.

Place chicken in a large bowl and season with spices and let marinate for 30 minutes in the refrigerator.

On a large cutting board place each chicken breast individually wrapping with plastic wrap and pounding to flatten just slightly.

Unwrap and place pre-made mashed potatoes in the middle of each chicken breast. Fold to close.

Place toothpick in middle of chicken to keep securely closed.

Sprinkle tops of stuffed chicken with cheddar cheese.

Place in greased 13 by 9 inch roasting pan. Bake for 40-45 minutes.

Serve with rice or your favourite pasta.

Chicken Soup Bake

Tastes like chicken soup but without the noodles!

1 lb chicken breasts, boneless
1 tbsp olive oil
1 onion, sliced into thin strips
1 cup baby carrots, chopped
1 cup celery, chopped
¾ cup corn, frozen
2 tbsp chicken bouillon base
1 can cream of celery soup
6 potatoes, medium
¼ cup milk
2 tbsp butter
2 tsp salt, more or less to taste

Slice chicken into thin slices.

In a large pot add olive oil and chicken cooking over medium heat until chicken is browned on all sides, stirring often.

Add in onions, carrots, celery, corn, bouillon base and soup mix, stirring for a minute over medium heat.

Transfer into a greased 13 by 9 inch casserole dish. Cover with tin foil. Bake in 375°F oven for 40 minutes or until vegetables are tender.

While this is baking, bring a large pot of water to a boil. Wash potatoes, peel and slice them and place in boiling water. Boil until tender. Drain and transfer to a large bowl.

Add milk, butter and salt. Mash potato mixture with a masher until fluffy and smooth, adding more or less milk and salt.

Once casserole is ready, top with mashed potatoes and smooth evenly.

Creamy Chicken and Rice

1 lb chicken breasts, boneless
1 tbsp olive oil
1 can cream of chicken soup mix
2 cups water
1 cup rice, long grain
1 cup mixed vegetables, frozen
¼ tsp pepper

Slice chicken into thin slices. In a large skillet, heat oil. Cook chicken until browned on all sides, stirring often. Set aside.

In a medium saucepan empty soup mix and water over medium heat. Stir and add rice, vegetables, and pepper. Add in cooked chicken, stirring well. Lower heat to low setting and stir occasionally until rice is cooked and creamy.

Chicken Rice and Peas

1 lb chicken breasts, boneless, sliced thinly
1 tbsp olive oil
2 cups rice
2 cups peas, frozen
5 cups water
1 tsp salt
½ tsp pepper
¼ tsp onion salt

In a large pot, heat oil. Cook chicken over medium heat until chicken is browned.

Add in rice, peas, water, salt, pepper and onion salt. Add more or less salt if needed. Mix and let cook until all the water has been absorbed and rice has cooked.

Chicken and Vegetable Layer - Maaloobi

This dish is a unique and flavourful one, great for a potluck!

1 chicken, skinned and cut up or 4 chicken breasts

10 cups water

2 cups vegetable oil, for frying

1 head cauliflower, pieces

1 eggplant, peeled and thinly sliced

3 cups rice, long grain

2 tbsp cinnamon

2 bay leaves

salt

In a large pot bring water to a boil. Add chicken cooking on medium heat for 45 minutes. Let cool. Debone chicken into bite size pieces, making sure to reserve chicken broth.

In a deep pot, place oil and heat until oil becomes very hot. Fry cauliflower pieces first, then eggplants. Transfer vegetables to a colander lined with paper towels to allow excess oil to be absorbed.

In a bowl wash rice, rinsing well.

In a large pot, layer chicken pieces on bottom, adding a bit of rice to cover the chicken.

Next layer the cauliflower and more rice to cover that layer, then the eggplant and the rest of rice. Place reserved chicken broth in a large bowl and add cinnamon and salt to taste, stir. Pour over layered casserole, pouring enough broth to cover rice. Add in bay leaves.

Cook over medium heat until all the chicken broth is absorbed and the rice has cooked.

To serve flip entire pot over large serving tray; remove pot and top with toasted pine nuts or toasted almonds.

Variation

Boneless beef pieces may be substituted for the chicken.

Maaloobi (Rice and Chicken) – Family Style

CHICKEN STOCK:

1 chicken, whole

cold water to cover chicken

1 onion, large

2 bay leaves

3 carrots, chopped

½ cup celery, chopped

¼ cup parsley

2 tsp salt

1 tsp black pepper

3 tbsp canola oil

In a large stock pot place all chicken broth ingredients and allow to simmer for 1 hour or until juices run clear. Remove chicken and shred into pieces; set aside. Strain the broth and discard the vegetables. To the warm broth, add the following ingredients and set aside:

2 cubes chicken bouillon

1 tsp black pepper

¼ tsp cayenne pepper

2 to 3 tsp curry powder

1 tbsp Vegeta food seasoning (optional)

3 tsp kabsah or biryani spice mix

1 tsp turmeric or a pinch of saffron strands

salt to taste

Tip

Kabsah or Biryani spice mix maybe found in most Middle Eastern grocery stores.

Maaloobi (Rice and Chicken) – Family Style continued

To assemble begin with…

1 onion, chopped
3 cloves garlic, minced
¼ to ½ cup olive oil
reserved shredded chicken
1 tsp turmeric
1 tsp black pepper
1 tsp seasoning salt
2 tsp curry powder
2 tsp kabsah or biryani spice mix
3 cups basmati rice - washed and drained
reserved chicken stock

In a large pot, add the chopped onion and olive oil, cook until onions are lightly browned, add the garlic and chicken, stir. Add turmeric, black pepper, seasoning salt, curry powder, Kabsah or biryani spice; stir well. Add the washed rice, DO NOT MIX.

Spread the rice over the chicken mixture. Add enough of the reserved chicken stock to cover the rice (about 1 cm above the rice).

Cover and cook on medium-high heat, once it comes to a boil, lower the heat to low and cook until broth has evaporated (about 20 to 25 minutes).

To serve, flip the entire pot over onto a large serving tray; remove pot and sprinkle with a ½ cup of pine nuts browned in a ¼ cup of butter.

Note

If you do not like pine nuts you may use any type of nut you desire.

Chicken Stir Fry

A great way to get your vegetables!

1 lb chicken breasts, boneless, thinly sliced

1 tbsp olive oil

1½ cups carrots, peeled and chopped

1½ cups cauliflower, pieced into bite size

1½ cups broccoli, cut into bite size

½ cup water

2 tbsp cornstarch

2 tbsp soy sauce

1 tsp browning sauce

2 tbsp Worchestershire sauce

1 tbsp garlic powder

1 tbsp salt

1 tsp seasoning salt

½ tsp pepper

In a large pot, heat oil. Cook chicken over medium heat until chicken is browned and cooked. Set aside.

Add carrots and cauliflower.

In a small bowl mix ½ cup of water and cornstarch, mixing well. Add this mixture to the chicken and vegetables. Let boil over medium heat.

Add in soy sauce, browning sauce, Worchestershire sauce and spices, adding more if needed. Let boil for approximately five minutes. Add in broccoli.

Continue boiling for another two minutes, making sure not to overcook the vegetables.

Serve over cooked rice or pasta.

Chicken Burgers

Great on the barbeque too!

1 egg
1 lb ground chicken
½ cup bread crumbs
2 tbsp parsley, chopped
½ tsp salt
¼ tsp pepper
1 tbsp vegetable oil

In a large bowl, beat egg; mix in chicken, crumbs, parsley, salt and pepper. Make into patties.

In large non-stick skillet heat oil over medium heat; cook patties for six minutes per side, until golden brown and no longer pink inside. Makes 5 burgers.

Chicken Fajitas

Fast and easy, a snap to make!

1 lb chicken breasts, boneless
1 tbsp olive oil
1 onion, thinly sliced
1 green pepper, thinly sliced
1 pkg fajita seasoning
¼ cup water

Slice chicken into thin pieces. In large non-stick skillet heat oil over medium heat; cook chicken until browned and no longer pink inside.

Add sliced vegetables. Add seasoning mixture and water. Coat and stir well. Cook for 5 minutes over low heat.

Spoon into tortilla wraps or pita bread. Top with salsa, lettuce, sour cream and shredded cheese.

Chicken Quesadillas

The kids are going to love these!

1 lb chicken breasts, boneless
10 flour tortillas, small
1 tsp olive oil
2 cups cheddar cheese, shredded
½ tsp margarine

Slice chicken into thin pieces. In large non-stick skillet heat oil over medium heat; cook chicken until browned and no longer pink. Pour into a bowl.

Place a couple of pieces of cooked chicken into a flour tortilla, filling only half the side. Top with cheese. Fold over.

In large non-stick skillet melt margarine. Place filled tortilla and cook on low heat, flipping when bottom is browned. Repeat. Makes ten.

Serve with salsa and sour cream.

If desired chopped vegetables can be added to the tortilla.

Chicken Bake Casserole

When you are in a hurry this one is just right to make!

1 cup rice, long grain

1½ cups vegetables, mixed frozen

1½ cups water

1 can cream of chicken soup

½ tsp seasoning salt

½ tsp garlic salt

4 chicken breasts, boneless

½ cup cheddar cheese, shredded

½ tsp black pepper

In a large mixing bowl mix rice, vegetables, water, soup mix and seasonings. Blend well. Pour into greased 13 by 9 inch casserole dish.

Arrange chicken breasts over rice mixture.

Cover with tin foil and bake in 375°F oven for 45 minutes.

Top with cheese and black pepper, allow the cheese to melt before serving.

Chicken Pot Pie

A great standby on those cold days!

¼ cup butter or margarine

¼ cup flour

1½ cups chicken broth (page 32)

¾ cup milk

½ tsp salt

¼ tsp pepper

1 cup carrots, sliced

1 cup peas, frozen

1 cup corn, frozen

1 onion, chopped

2 cups chicken, cooked and cubed

2 pie crusts, prepared

Preheat oven to 400°F. Melt butter in a saucepan over medium heat. Stir in flour, broth, milk, salt and pepper. Cook, stirring constantly until mixture is bubbly.

Stir in carrots, peas, corn, onion and chicken; boil for one minute. Set aside.

Prepare pie crusts. Roll pastry and place in a greased baking dish.

Pour chicken filling over crust. Top with second crust.

Turn edges of pastry under and flute. Design top crust as desired.

Bake for 40 minutes or until golden brown.

Chicken Souvlaki

Chicken kabobs wrapped in flavour!

1 lb chicken breasts, boneless
2 tbsp olive oil
1 tbsp oregano
½ lemon, squeezed
2 tsp seasoning salt
2 cloves garlic, crushed
¼ tsp pepper

Cut chicken into 2-inch chunks. Place in a large bowl, adding oil, oregano, lemon juice, garlic and seasonings. Cover and marinate for one hour. Thread chicken pieces onto skewers. Broil, barbeque or place on greased grill over medium heat; cook turning every 4 minutes, for 12 minutes or until no longer pink.

TZATZIKI SAUCE

1 English cucumber, small
½ tsp salt
1½ cups yogurt, plain
1 tbsp mint, dried
1 tsp dill, dried
1 clove garlic, crushed
¼ cup water
pita bread
lettuce, tomatoes, onions

To make sauce, shred cucumber. In a mixing bowl add shredded cucumber and the rest of the ingredients for the sauce. Blend well. Refrigerate until use.

Cut pitas in half; open to form pockets. Slide chicken skewers into pita pockets and top with sauce, sliced tomatoes, lettuce and chopped onions.

Mloukiah

This is exceptionally good if you have a cold!

1 lb Mloukiah, dry

4 cups water, hot

1 chicken, whole, skinless

8 cups water

1 onion

2 bay leaves

3 tbsp olive oil

5 garlic cloves, diced

2 bunches cilantro

1 lemon, squeezed

1 tsp lemon salt

½ tsp pepper

2 tsp salt

1 tomato

In a large bowl soak Mloukiah with the hot water for 30 minutes. Set aside.

In a large pot over medium heat bring water to a boil and add chicken, onion and bay leaves. Let cook for about 45 minutes or until chicken is fully cooked. If more water is needed during boiling add more in the pot.

Take chicken and debone the chicken into bite size pieces making sure to reserve the chicken stock and onion. Discard bay leaves.

Take the onion and chop it finely.

Drain the Mloukiah and rinse with cold water in a colander. Squeeze dry.

In a large pot over medium heat add olive oil, chopped onion, garlic, Mloukiah, cilantro, lemon juice and lemon salt. Let cook for two minutes.

Add the reserved chicken stock and the chicken pieces. Mix in pepper and salt.

Add more salt if needed.

Cut tomato in half and add to pot. Gently boil for 20 minutes, stirring occasionally.

Before serving remove tomato pieces and discard.

Serve over rice.

Mloukiah can be found in any Middle Eastern Grocery Store. Mloukiah is a long, leafy vegetable, grown mainly in Egypt. It may be found in dry form or frozen.

Mloukiah with Chicken

This is another version!

CHICKEN STOCK:

1 kg chicken breasts (with bone in) *or*
1 whole chicken

10 cups water

1 onion

½ cup carrots

½ cup celery

bay leaves

¼ cup parsley

2 tsp salt

1 tsp pepper

INGREDIENTS NEEDED TO ASSEMBLE:

½ cup olive oil

1 large onion, chopped

6 cloves garlic, minced

½ cup parsley, chopped

½ cup cilantro, chopped

1 tsp seasoning salt

½ tsp cinnamon

1 tsp black pepper

3 tsp salt or to taste

2 cubes chicken bouillon

4 packages frozen Mloukiah, thawed

2 lemons, squeezed

Place chicken in a stockpot; pour cold water to cover the chicken. Add the carrots, celery, onion, parsley, bay leaves, salt and pepper. Boil until chicken is cooked through, about 1 hour. Remove the chicken from liquid and allow to cool; debone chicken into bite size pieces, set aside. Strain and reserve the chicken stock, add the 2 cubes of chicken bouillon to the hot chicken stock, set aside.

In a large pot, add the onions and olive oil. Cook on medium high heat until onions are lightly browned. Add the garlic and stir, once the aroma of garlic is present add the reserved pieced chicken, stir. Add the parsley, cilantro, seasoning salt, cinnamon, black pepper, and salt; stir. Add the Mloukiah and enough of the reserved chicken stock to make the mixture into the consistency of a thick soup. If you like it to be thicker, add less liquid stock and if you like it thinner add more liquid stock. Stir and taste, adjust seasonings to your liking. Add the lemon juice and bring to a boil, stirring occasionally.

Serve with rice and lemon wedges.

Lebanese Seasoned Baked Chicken

1 kg chicken pieces

4 potatoes, cubed

3 large onions, coarsely chopped

½ cup olive oil

3 tsp cinnamon

1 tsp allspice

½ tsp black pepper

2 tsp salt

2 tsp Sumac (optional)

Preheat oven to 425° F.

In a food processor, add the coarsely chopped onions and process until mixture is finely chopped. Remove and place in a mixing bowl. Add the olive oil, cinnamon, allspice, black pepper, salt and sumac; mix well.

In a large mixing bowl, add the chicken pieces and cubed potatoes. Add the onion mixture and rub well over the chicken and potatoes. Place mixture in a baking pan and bake in oven until golden brown or until chicken juices run clear, approximately 1 hour.

Serve with green salad and favourite steamed vegetables.

Grilled Chicken Breasts

1 kg chicken breasts – boneless and skinless

½ cup olive oil

4 cloves garlic, crushed

1 jalapeño pepper, minced

2 tsp seasoning salt

3 tsp Montreal chicken seasoning (no salt)

1 tsp black pepper

dash liquid smoke

2 lemons, squeezed

In a large mixing bowl add the chicken and the remainder of ingredients; mix well. Marinate for ½ an hour to 1 hour.

Grill chicken on BBQ until well done.

Serve with salad, hummus dip and pita bread.

Baked and Breaded Chicken

1 kg chicken – skinless

½ cup olive oil

4 cloves garlic, crushed

1 jalapeño pepper, minced

2 tsp seasoning salt

3 tsp Montreal chicken seasoning (no salt)

1 tsp black pepper

dash liquid smoke

2 lemons, squeezed

4 envelopes chicken coating

½ cup butter, melted

Preheat oven to 425°F.

In a large mixing bowl add the chicken and the remainder of ingredients except chicken coating and butter; mix well. Marinate for ½ an hour to 1 hour.

In a large Ziploc bag, pour the chicken coating into the bag. Place a few pieces of chicken into the bag and coat with the mixture. Repeat with remaining chicken pieces; place each piece of chicken on a baking tray. Drizzle with melted butter and bake until golden brown and well cooked.

Serve with mashed potatoes and steamed vegetables.

Chicken Pansett - Stir-Fry

CHICKEN MARINADE:

In a large bowl combine the following 9 ingredients and marinate for 1 hour...

1 kg chicken breast (boneless and skinless), sliced into thin strips

¼ cup orange juice

2 tsp seasoning salt

1 tsp black pepper

1 tbsp worchestershire sauce

2 tbsp soya sauce

½ tsp garlic powder

½ tsp ginger powder or 1 tsp fresh ginger grated

1 bottle orange/ginger marinade

VEGETABLES: *(you may omit or add any vegetables you wish)*

1 large onion, thinly sliced

2 cups mushrooms, sliced

1 cup green pepper, julienned

1 cup snow peas

2 cups carrots, sliced

2 cups bean sprouts

1 cup broccoli, chopped

SAUCE:

2 cups cold water

3 tbsp cornstarch

2 tbsp soya sauce

1 tbsp worchestershire sauce

1 tsp black pepper

½ tsp seasoning salt

1 to 2 tsp browning sauce

Mix sauce ingredients and set aside.

In a large skillet or wok, heat a ¼ cup of olive oil, add the chicken mixture and cook until chicken is tender and cooked through. Add your choice of vegetables and stir. Add sauce and stir. Cook until sauce comes to a boil. Taste and adjust seasoning to your liking.

Serve with Basmati rice if not making Pansett.

TO MAKE PANSETT: Cook 1 package of rice noodles according to package directions. Drain and run knife through the noodles to cut into smaller pieces. Add noodles to the stir-fry mixture and mix well. Serve and enjoy with soya sauce or lemon wedges.

Variation

Instead of chicken you may substitute it for beef, prawns or squid following the same directions.

Chicken in a Mushroom Cream Sauce

6 chicken breasts

4 cloves garlic, minced

1 tsp black pepper

2 tsp salt

1 lemon, squeezed

3 tbsp coriander, chopped

4 tbsp olive oil

SAUCE:

3 tbsp butter

1 onion, finely chopped

4 cloves garlic, halved

1 package mushrooms, sliced

1 tsp mustard powder

2 tsp chicken bouillon

1 - 250g pkg sour cream

¾ cup whipping cream

In a large mixing bowl, slice the chicken breasts in half, lengthwise and add the garlic, black pepper, salt, lemon juice, and coriander; set aside to marinate for 1 hour.

In a skillet, add olive oil and chicken pieces. Cook until golden brown on both sides and chicken is cooked through and no longer pink. Set aside.

To make the sauce, in a large pot, add the butter and onions, cook until the onions are lightly browned. Add the garlic and mushrooms. Cook for 2 minutes. Add the mustard powder, chicken bouillon, sour cream and whipping cream. Cook over low heat for 5 minutes. Add the cooked chicken pieces and cook for an additional 5 minutes.

Serve over rice or noodles.

Variation

Chicken may be cut into strips or smaller bite sized pieces.

Roasted, Glazed Chicken

1 whole chicken, cleaned and pat dried

GLAZE:
½ cup orange juice

2 tbsp grainy mustard

2 tbsp honey

¼ tsp ground cloves

¼ tsp cinnamon

STUFFING:
2 apples, coarsely chopped

2 oranges, coarsely chopped

6 rosemary springs, fresh

1 tsp salt

1 tsp pepper

Preheat oven to 400°F.

Sprinkle salt and pepper over chicken and inside of cavity. Stuff chicken with coarsely chopped apples and oranges with peel; add rosemary springs.

In a mixing bowl, combine glaze ingredients and spread over the chicken and drizzle some glaze inside of cavity. Save remaining glaze. Place the chicken in a roasting pan and place in the oven.

Glaze (use the remainder of the glaze) and baste the chicken every 15 minutes. Bake for 1 to 1½ hours or until juices run clear and golden brown.

Note

If chicken browns too quickly, cover with foil and continue with directions.

Lebanese Style Chicken Rolls

ROAST CHICKEN:

1 chicken, whole

1 onion, coarsely chopped

1 bay leaf

2 cloves garlic

salt

pepper

olive oil

FILLING:

3 to 4 onions, chopped

¾ to 1 cup olive oil

1 tsp black pepper

1 tsp salt

3 tsp sumac

½ tsp cinnamon

½ tsp allspice

deboned and chopped roast chicken

Lebanese sajj bread or pita bread

Preheat oven to 400°F.

Clean and pat dry the chicken. Sprinkle and rub with salt, pepper and drizzle with olive oil over chicken. Inside of cavity, stuff with 1 coarsely chopped onion, bay leaf, 2 cloves of garlic and a drizzle of olive oil. Place whole chicken in a roasting pan. Roast chicken for 1½ hours or until cooked through and juices run clear when a knife is inserted in the thickest part of the chicken. When cool enough to handle, debone chicken and chop chicken into small pieces; set aside.

To make the filling, place chopped onions and olive oil in a large pot. Cook until onions are wilted and lightly browned. Add the black pepper, salt, sumac, cinnamon, and allspice; stir and add chopped roasted chicken. Taste and adjust seasoning to your liking. Set aside.

Using the Lebanese Sajj Bread, cut bread into rectangles about the size of your hand; place 1 heaping tablespoon of filling and spread lengthwise at one end. Roll the bread over the filling and continue to roll, jelly roll style. Continue with the remaining bread and filling.

Note: If Lebanese Sajj bread can not be found you may use Pita bread or Tortilla bread.

Lebanese Sajj bread is a thin and versatile type of bread that can be found in Mediterranean food stores.

Chicken Broccoli Fettuccine

½ pkg fettuccine

8 cups water

pinch salt

1 cup broccoli, chopped

1 lb chicken breast

1 tbsp olive oil

2 cans cream of mushroom soup

½ cup milk

2 tbsp Parmesan cheese

½ tsp pepper

Bring water to a boil in a large pot. Add pinch of salt. Then add fettuccine. Cook as directed on package, trying not to overcook the pasta. Add broccoli to the pasta when there is only three minutes left to cook. Drain pasta and broccoli, set aside.

Cut chicken breast into thin slices. In a large pot heat olive oil and add chicken breast. Cook until the chicken is well done and slightly browned. Add in soup mixture and milk. Stir well. Add in cheese and pepper. Let boil. Then add fettuccine and broccoli, coating well. Serve immediately.

Chicken and Linguine

So easy and so satisfying!

4 chicken breasts
seasoning salt
10 cups water
¼ tsp salt
1 pkg (375g) linguine pasta, whole wheat
1 jar favourite pasta sauce
Parmesan cheese

Heat oven to 400°F. Place chicken breasts in a baking casserole dish. Sprinkle with seasoning salt; cover with tin foil. Bake for 30 minutes.

In a large pot add water and salt; bring to a boil over medium heat. Once it begins to boil add pasta and cook according to package directions. Drain pasta. Set aside.

In a small saucepan pour pasta sauce and heat over low heat until it boils. Set aside.

Once chicken has cooked slice the chicken into thin strips.

To assemble dish, pour linguine in a large pasta dish topping it with the chicken pieces and sauce. Top with Parmesan cheese and eat right away.

Serve with garlic bread.

Meats

Roast Beef

1–2 kg beef roast
6 cloves garlic
¼ cup olive oil
1 tsp salt
2 tsp black pepper
4 tsp Montreal steak spice
6 celery, cut in half
6 carrots, cut in half
4 potatoes, peeled and quartered
2 onions, quartered
olive oil
salt and pepper

Preheat oven to 350°F.

With a knife, pierce meat. Insert 1 clove of garlic. Repeat with remaining garlic, piercing meat in various places.

Rub olive oil, salt, pepper and steak spice all over meat. Place meat in a roasting pan. Set aside.

In a bowl, add the celery, carrots, potatoes and onions. Rub olive oil, salt, and pepper over the vegetables, mix well. Arrange vegetables around the roast. Place in oven.

Do not cover.

For medium rare cook until meat thermometer reaches 160°F.

For well done, cook until meat thermometer reaches 170°F.

Remove from oven, cover loosely and allow meat to rest for 10- 15 minutes. This allows for easier carving. Slice and serve.

(See picture at beginning of the chapter)

Meat Kabobs

1 kg beef or lamb cubes- choose tender cuts of meat

¼ cup olive oil

2 tsp salt

1 tsp black pepper

3 tsp Montreal steak spice

dash cayenne pepper (optional)

1 onion, quartered

1 green pepper, quartered

1 tomato, quartered

10-15 whole mushrooms (optional)

bamboo meat skewers

Soak meat skewers in water for 30 minutes.

In a large bowl, add meat, olive oil, salt, black pepper, Montreal steak spice and cayenne pepper. Rub well.

Start by taking 1 meat skewer and alternate by piercing the meat and vegetables into the skewer. Repeat until all the meat and vegetables are used up.

Heat BBQ and place skewers on hot grill. Cook until desired doneness is reached remembering to rotate during cooking.

Burgers

1 kg ground beef

1 package onion soup mix

2 tbsp worchestershire sauce

¼ cup olive oil

½ cup parsley, chopped fine

¼ cup mint, chopped fine or 2 tbsp dried mint

1 onion, grated

dash liquid smoke

1½ tsp salt

1 tsp black pepper

2 tsp Montreal steak spice

In a large bowl add all the ingredients and mix well.

Make into patties. Preheat BBQ to medium.

Cook burgers on greased grill for 5 to 7 minutes per side, and internal temperature of beef reaches 160°F. Transfer to a large plate and keep warm.

Serve on a bun with your favourite toppings.

Kafta

This is a Lebanese meat loaf!

2 lbs ground beef
1 onion, grated
1 tsp salt
¼ tsp black pepper
1 tsp garlic powder
¼ tsp allspice
½ cup parsley, chopped fine
¼ cup barbeque sauce

In a mixing bowl add all the ingredients, and mix well until blended.

Pour into a casserole dish, spreading evenly. Cover with tin foil.

Bake in oven at 400°F for 40 to 50 minutes or until cooked, making sure not to overcook.

Serve with rice and salad.

Variation

(1) Can be barbequed. Place on skewers and BBQ as kabobs.

(2) Can be baked as individual pieces. Form into small long or round rolls and place on a greased cookie sheet and bake in oven at 400°F for 30 minutes, or until cooked through. Can be used for a pita stuffing and topped with vegetables and dressing of choice.

Kafta with Potatoes

Meatloaf with potatoes!

2 lbs ground beef

1 onion, grated

1 tsp salt

¼ tsp black pepper

1 tsp garlic powder

¼ tsp allspice

½ cup parsley, finely chopped

4 potatoes

1 cup tomato sauce

1 tsp seasoning salt

In mixing bowl add ground beef, onion, salt, pepper, garlic powder, allspice and parsley.

Mix well until blended.

Pour into a casserole dish, spreading evenly.

Peel potatoes and wash and slice into 1 inch thick slices.

Place potato slices on top of meat. Pour tomato sauce over potatoes evenly and sprinkle with seasoning salt. Cover with tin foil.

Bake in oven at 400°F for 40 to 50 minutes or until meat is cooked and potatoes are tender. Serve over rice if desired.

Beef Stir Fry

A great way to get your vegetables!

1 lb beef, sirloin, thinly sliced

2 garlic cloves, crushed

2 tbsp ginger, minced

¼ cup orange juice

2 tbsp worchestershire sauce

4 tbsp soya sauce

1-2 tsp salt

1 tsp pepper

1 bottle stir-fry marinade

1½ cups water

2 tbsp cornstarch

1 red onion, thinly sliced

1 pkg mushrooms, thinly sliced

1 green pepper, thinly sliced

1-2 cups snap or snow peas

2 cups carrots, thinly sliced

2 cups bean sprouts

1 cup broccoli, chopped into small pieces

In a large bowl marinate first nine ingredients for 30 minutes.

In a large pot over medium heat, cook the first nine ingredients until the meat is browned and cooked.

In a small bowl mix water and cornstarch, stirring well making sure there is no lumps.

Add this to the meat mixture and let it come to a gentle boil.

Add in onions, mushrooms, peppers, peas and carrots. Stir well making sure to coat the vegetables. Let boil for 5 minutes or until vegetables are tender crisp.

Add in bean sprouts and broccoli, only boil for 2 extra minutes.

Serve over rice or prepared Chinese noodles.

You can add as many different kinds of vegetables, just use your imagination!

Tacos

The kids will love this one!

1 lb ground beef
1 cup water
4 tbsp taco seasoning
12 taco shells or tortilla wraps (6)
½ head iceberg lettuce, shredded
2 tomatoes, diced
2 cups cheddar cheese, shredded
sour cream
salsa

In a saucepan cook ground beef over medium heat until browned and drain off fat.

Stir in water and taco seasonings. Bring to a boil and simmer uncovered for 10 minutes on low heat. Stir occasionally.

Heat taco shells in oven at 350°F for five minutes. Let cool.

Spoon meat into taco shells and top with lettuce, tomatoes, cheese, sour cream, and salsa.

If using wraps, spoon meat into wraps and top with lettuce, tomatoes, cheese, sour cream and salsa. Enjoy!

Chili Stir Fry

1 tsp olive oil

½ lb lean ground beef

1 tsp olive oil

1 large onion, chopped

2 tsp chili powder

½ tsp seasoning salt

⅛ tsp cayenne pepper

1 – 14 oz can tomatoes, diced, drained and ¼ cup juice reserved

2 – 14 oz can kidney beans, drained

1 tsp sugar

3 cups prepared rice

In a large pot on medium heat add olive oil and ground beef. Cook until browned and cooked through, drain liquid. Transfer to a bowl.

Add second amount of olive oil in the same pot. Add the onion, chili powder, seasoning salt and cayenne pepper. Stir for two minutes on low heat or until onion is browned.

Add the cooked beef, tomatoes, tomato juice reserve, kidney beans, and sugar. Stir well and let boil for five minutes.

Serve over cooked rice.

Cabbage Rolls

Tasty and delicious!

8 cups water
1 cabbage, head
1½ cups rice, calrose style
1 cup ground beef, cooked
2 tomatoes, finely diced
½ cup parsley, finely chopped
2 tbsp mint, dried
2 tsp salt, or more if needed
¼ tsp black pepper
1 tsp seasoning salt
¼ cup olive oil
water

In a large pot bring water to a boil. Cut the bottom of the cabbage and core out a little of the middle from the bottom. Put cabbage into the boiling water. The leaves should fall off easily. Take each cabbage leaf off, one by one. Drain and let cool.

In a mixing bowl, wash rice. Add meat, tomatoes, parsley, mint, salt, black pepper, seasoning salt, and olive oil. Mix well.

Place in each cabbage a tablespoonful of the filling and roll lengthwise. Arrange in a large pot with the first row going one way and the next going the opposite way, so the cabbage rolls crisscross. Repeat this step until all the cabbage rolls are done.

Place an oven proof flat dish on top of the cabbage rolls in the pot. This will allow the cabbage rolls to stay put. Add enough water in the pot to cover cabbage rolls and gently cook on medium-low heat for about an hour and a half until the rice is tender. Remove plate and let cook for ten minutes more or until all the water is evaporated.

Stuffed Zucchini __
Koussa Mihshee

12 zucchinis, small

1 cup calrose rice, rinsed and drained

½ cup ground beef, cooked

1 tsp salt

¼ tsp pepper

½ tsp seasoning salt

¼ tsp cinnamon

1 tsp mint, dried

¼ cup olive oil

2 potatoes, thickly sliced

2 tomatoes, sliced

cold water

SAUCE

2 cups tomato sauce

1 tsp seasoning salt

3 cloves fresh garlic, crushed

Wash zucchini and hollow out the insides of the zucchini. Remove the insides of the zucchini by using a knife or a zucchini corer, making sure not to core too much. Also try not to pierce the walls of the zucchini. Save the insides to be used in other zucchini recipes. Place hollowed out zucchini in a large bowl filled with cold, salted water. Rinse each zucchini in the salted water and place opening down on a tray to drain.

In a large bowl wash rice well and rinse. Add ground beef, salt, pepper, seasoning salt, cinnamon, mint, and olive oil. Mix well.

Take hollowed zucchini and stuff with rice mixture filling only three quarters of the way. Repeat this step for all the zucchini.

In a large stockpot, layer the potatoes and tomatoes. Place the stuffed zucchini on top of the vegetables in a circular pattern, close together.

Once complete, place an oven proof flat dish over the stuffed zucchini (this will help keep the zucchini in place) pour enough cold water over the zucchini until covered, about 1 inch above the zucchini. Bring to a boil, reduce heat and allow to simmer.

In a large bowl add tomato sauce, seasoning salt, and garlic. Stir.

Gently pour tomato sauce over the zucchini and cook over medium heat for one hour or until the stuffing has cooked and is soft. Remove zucchini from tomato broth.

It is important to remove the zucchinis from the tomato broth as soon as the zucchini are fully cooked because if you leave the zucchinis in the tomato broth while cooling, the shells of the zucchini will crack and split open. To serve, place zucchini in a serving platter topped with the tomato broth.

Green Bean Stew

This is extremely delicious when using the freshest ingredients!

2 tbsp olive oil

1 onion, diced

1 lb beef, sirloin or any tender meat

3 tomatoes, diced

2 cups green beans, fresh or frozen

4 cups water

¼ cup tomato paste

1 tsp salt

¼ tsp black pepper

1 garlic clove, crushed

In a large pot heat olive oil on medium heat, add in onion. Cook until limp and slightly browned. Cut beef into half-inch cubes and add to the onions. Cook meat until browned.

If using fresh beans wash and tear ends off and cut into bite sized pieces.

Add tomatoes, green beans, water, tomato paste, salt, pepper, and garlic.

Boil over medium heat, stirring constantly. Add more seasonings if needed.

Cook until the green beans are tender. Serve over rice.

Kidney Bean Stew

This is another way to make chili!

2 tbsp olive oil

1 onion, diced

1lb beef, sirloin or any tender meat

2 - 14 oz cans red kidney beans, or any type of beans

¼ cup tomato paste

4 cups water

1 garlic clove, crushed

1 tsp salt

¼ tsp black pepper

½ tsp seasoning salt

In a large pot heat olive oil on medium heat, add diced onion. Cook onion until limp and slightly browned. Cut beef into half-inch thick cubes and add to the onions. Cook meat until browned.

Add in kidney beans, tomato paste, water, garlic, salt, pepper, and seasoning salt.

Stir and cook for about 20 minutes until sauce thickens.

Add more water if needed.

Variation

Ground beef could be used instead of the stewing beef cubes. Serve over rice if desired.

Okra Stew - Bami

Eaman's Special, dedicated to my mother-in-law, Aminah Omar, who was a constant source of inspiration.

1 cup canola oil

2 lbs okra, fresh or frozen

1 potato, diced small

1 tsp lemon salt

2 tbsp margarine

¼ cup canola oil

1 lb beef, sirloin, cut into bite sized chunks

2 garlic cloves, crushed

1 bunch cilantro, finely chopped

4 cups water

¼ cup tomato paste

¼ tsp cayenne pepper

¼ tsp black pepper

salt to taste

In a large pot heat 1 cup of canola oil. When hot enough fry okra until lightly browned.

Line a plate with paper towels. Transfer the okra into the plate.

Next fry the potatoes until lightly browned. Transfer the potatoes into another paper towel lined plate.

Sprinkle both the okra and potatoes with lemon salt. Let sit for 5 minutes.

In a large pot heat over medium heat the margarine and canola oil. Add in the beef chunks and garlic. Cook until the meat is browned and cooked.

Add in cilantro, water, tomato paste, peppers, and salt. Bring to a boil over medium heat.

Add in the okra and potatoes. Stir and boil for another 10 minutes so all the flavours blend together.

Serve over rice.

Shepherd's Pie

What real comfort food should taste like!

1 tsp olive oil

1 lb lean ground beef

1 large onion, chopped

1 tbsp flour

1 tsp salt

¼ tsp pepper

½ cup milk

2 cups mixed vegetables, cooked

1 tbsp ketchup or tomato paste

1 tsp worchestershire sauce

Mashed potatoes:

water - enough to cover potatoes

6 large potatoes, peeled and cut up

¼ cup milk

1 tbsp butter

2 tsp salt

Topping

2 tbsp butter, melted

In a large pot on medium heat, add olive oil, ground beef and onion. Cook until meat is browned and cooked through and onion is limp. Drain any liquid.

Add flour, salt, and pepper. Stir well. Add ½ cup milk and let boil on medium heat for two minutes until thickened.

Add vegetables, ketchup and Worchestershire sauce. Stir and boil for another minute.

Spread evenly in casserole dish.

Cook potatoes in water in a large pot until tender. Drain and place in large bowl. Add milk, butter, and salt. Mash until smooth. Spread on top of beef mixture.

Brush potatoes with melted butter.

Bake in oven uncovered at 350°F for 30 minutes.

Meat Maaloobi

This is a meat and rice casserole!

1 kg beef or lamb, cut into large pieces or large cubes

cold water- enough to cover meat

2 bay leaves

3 tsp salt

2 tsp black pepper

2 carrots, coarsely chopped

2 celery stalks, coarsely chopped

2 tbsp olive oil

¼ cup parsley springs

ASSEMBLE:

1 large onion, chopped

¼ cup olive oil

4 cloves garlic, minced

1 tsp turmeric

1 tsp biryani spice mix

½ tsp black pepper

3 cups basmati rice, washed and rinsed

ADD TO THE COOKED BROTH :

salt to taste

1 tsp black pepper

2 tsp turmeric

1-2 tsp allspice

3 tsp biryani spice mix (optional)

2 cubes beef bouillon

Place first nine ingredients in a large pot. Bring to a boil over medium heat. Remove any foam. Lower heat, cover and simmer for 1- 1½ hours or until meat is tender. Remove meat from broth and place meat in a large bowl.

Strain broth and discard vegetables.

Add the spices to the broth and set aside.

In a large stockpot on medium heat, add onion, olive oil, and garlic.

Cook until lightly browned. Add the meat pieces and turmeric, biryani spice mix and black pepper; stir well.

Spread rice evenly over meat. Pour enough reserved broth over rice until broth reaches

2 cm above rice. Do not stir.

Cover and bring to a boil and lower heat to low and simmer. Cook until broth is absorbed and rice is tender about 20- 25 minutes.

Turn the whole pot onto a large deep serving pan. Sprinkle with ½ cup toasted pine nuts or almonds and ¼ cup golden raisins if desired.

Lasagne

1 package lasagne noodles – cooked- follow directions on package

¼ cup olive oil

1 large onion, finely chopped

4 cloves garlic, crushed

2 lbs ground beef

1 green pepper, diced fine

2 cups mushrooms, sliced

2 - 14 oz cans tomato sauce

1 can water

2 tsp oregano

1 tsp thyme

1 tsp basil

1 tsp seasoning salt

salt to taste

½ tsp black pepper

1 tsp Mexican chili powder

4-6 cups shredded mozzarella cheese

12 cheese, slices

½ cup Parmesan cheese

Cook lasagne noodles according to package directions, drain and set aside.

In a large pot add olive oil, onions, garlic and ground beef. Cook on medium heat until meat has cooked through and onion is limp. Add green peppers and mushrooms. Cook for two minutes. Add the tomato sauce, water and all the seasonings. Let boil for 15 minutes on low heat, stirring occasionally. Set aside.

To assemble, layer ingredients in greased large lasagne pan.

Start with a bit of the tomato-meat sauce being poured on the bottom of the dish.

Layer lasagne noodles, slightly overlapping to fit the dish. Top with tomato-meat sauce and spread evenly. Top with some shredded mozzarella and cheese slices to cover layer. Then top with more lasagne noodles. Repeat these steps for each layer, ending with the cheese layer. Top with mozzarella and Parmesan cheese.

Bake covered with foil in 350°F oven for 30 minutes, then remove foil and allow to bake for another 30 minutes or until cheese is bubbly and browned.

Spaghetti

spaghetti – cooked according to package directions

¼ cup olive oil

1 large onion, chopped

4 cloves garlic, minced

½ kg ground beef

½ green pepper, chopped fine

1 cup mushrooms, sliced

6 large tomatoes, peeled and pureed, or 2 - 14 oz cans tomato sauce

1 - 5.5 oz can tomato paste

1½ cups water, you may add more water if you prefer a thinner consistency

2-3 tsp sugar

3 tsp oregano

2 tsp basil

2 tsp thyme

2 tsp salt or to taste

2 tsp black pepper

3 tsp Mexican chili powder (optional)

Parmesan cheese, (optional)

Cook spaghetti according to package, drain and set aside.

In a large pot add olive oil, onion, garlic, and ground beef over medium heat. Cook until meat has browned and cooked through and onions are limp. Add in green peppers and mushrooms. Cook for two minutes.

Add in the rest of the ingredients except for the Parmesan cheese, stirring occasionally. Let boil on low heat for 15 minutes.

Spaghetti can be mixed into the sauce or topped with the sauce.

Sprinkle with Parmesan if desired.

Rotini in a Pan

4 cups rotini pasta (any other type of pasta could be used)

6 cups water

2 tbsp olive oil

2 tbsp olive oil

1 onion, grated or chopped

1 garlic clove, crushed

½ kg ground beef

1 tbsp steak spice

1 green pepper, diced

1 celery, diced

10 mushrooms, diced

2 cans tomato sauce (a 398ml and a 213ml)

1½ can water (use the 398ml can)

1 tsp salt

½ tsp pepper

2 tbsp oregano (ground or leaves)

2 tbsp parsley, fresh or dried

6 cheese slices, light

1 cup grated light mozzarella cheese

1 cup grated light cheddar cheese

¼ cup light Parmesan cheese

In a large pot bring water to a boil and add the first amount of olive oil. Add pasta and cook for about 14 minutes or until pasta is tender. Drain pasta into a strainer and run under cold water to prevent pasta from sticking together.

Put second amount of olive oil in a pot on medium heat. Add onion, garlic, and ground beef. Be sure to keep stirring so ground beef does not stick.

Add steak spice to beef mixture. Once the beef is cooked add the green pepper, celery, and mushrooms.

Cook for about five minutes then add the tomato sauce, water, salt, pepper, oregano, and parsley.

Cover and let boil for about 15-20 minutes on low heat. Taste the sauce to make sure the spices are as desired. Stir the sauce to make sure the sauce is not too thick and not too runny.

Once the sauce is ready, add the pasta and cook for another 5 minutes on low heat.

Take a 13 by 9 inch pan and spread out half of the pasta.

Take 3 of the cheese slices and cut in half and lay over the pasta.

Take one handful of the shredded cheeses and lightly sprinkle over pasta layer.

Layer the other half of the pasta and spread evenly.

Lay the other 3 cheese slices on top of the pasta and cover with the rest of the grated cheese. Top with Parmesan Cheese.

Bake in 375°F oven, uncovered for about 20-30 minutes or until lightly browned.

Kibbi Nayeh – Meat with crushed wheat

cold water

¾ cup fine crushed wheat (burghul or bulgar)

1 kg extra lean ground beef or kibbi meat

1 onion, grated fine

1 tsp salt or to taste

2 tsp cumin

½ tsp black pepper

½ tsp allspice (optional)

1 tsp dried mint

2 tsp marjoram

¼ cup olive oil

ice water or very cold water (used for dipping)

Soak the crushed wheat in cold water in large bowl for five minutes. Drain.

Add the ground beef, grated onion, salt, cumin, black pepper, allspice, dried mint and marjoram. Knead well, dipping hands in cold water. Once mixed well, add olive oil and knead.

Transfer the kibbi to a serving platter, and flatten slightly, making the shape of the platter and smooth all over with hands. Using a fork or a spoon, make a pattern. Decorate with parsley. Serve with olive oil on the side or on the top.

Stuffed Kibbi Balls

5 cups fine crushed wheat (burghul or bulgar)

1 kg extra lean ground beef or kibbi meat

1 onion, grated

2 tsp salt or to taste

1 tsp black pepper

2 tsp marjoram

3 tsp dried mint

4 tsp ground cumin

1 tsp allspice (optional)

ice water or very cold water

KIBBI MEAT STUFFING

$1/3$ cup olive oil

4-6 large onions, diced small

1 kg ground beef

2 tsp black pepper

1 tsp seasoning salt

¼ tsp cinnamon

2-3 tsp cumin

2 tsp allspice

3-4 tsp sumac

4 tsp Mexican chili powder (optional)

salt to taste

1 cup toasted pine nuts

In large bowl soak crushed wheat with cold water. Let stand for five minutes and drain.

Add meat, onion, salt, black pepper, marjoram, dried mint, and cumin. Mix well with hands. If mixture is not pliable, add cold water a little at a time when mixing.

Run the mixture through a food processor, a little at a time. Set aside.

To prepare filling, cook oil, onions, and ground beef in a frying pan, on medium heat. Cook until onions are limp and meat is cooked. Add the rest of the ingredients. Mix and let cool for 5 minutes.

With wet hands, take a small piece of the kibbi mixture and roll into a ball, the size of a golf ball. With the ball in one hand, place finger of the other hand in middle rotating the ball evenly to make the hole larger until you have a thin shell. Place a tablespoon of the filling and then close the ball by bringing the open end of the ball together, using some water on finger tips. The shape should resemble a sphere. Repeat for all the kibbi balls and place on a tray until ready to fry. Also could be barbequed.

Deep fry in vegetable or canola oil, until golden brown. Place on a paper towel lined plate. Serve warm.

Baked Kibbi

3 cups fine crushed wheat (burghul or bulgar)

1 kg extra lean ground beef or kibbi meat

1 onion, finely grated

2 tsp salt or to taste

1 tsp black pepper

1 tsp marjoram

1 tsp dried mint

2 tsp ground cumin

1 tsp allspice (optional)

ice water or very cold water

3 tbsp melted butter

KIBBI MEAT FILLING

¼ cup olive oil

2 large onions, diced small

½ kg ground beef

½ tsp black pepper

1 tsp seasoning salt

2 tsp parsley, dried

1 tsp cumin

½ tsp allspice

½ tsp Mexican chili powder (optional)

salt to taste

½ cup toasted pine nuts

In large bowl soak crushed wheat with cold water. Let stand for five minutes and drain.

Add meat, onion, salt, black pepper, marjoram, dried mint, allspice and cumin. Mix well with hands. If mixture is not pliable, add cold water a little at a time when mixing. Set aside.

To prepare filling, cook oil, onions, and ground beef in a frying pan, on medium heat. Cook until onions are limp and meat is cooked. Add the rest of the ingredients. Mix and let cool for 5 minutes.

Preheat oven to 400°F. In a large greased casserole dish spread evenly half of kibbi mixture and then pour and spread filling on top.

Layer with the other half of the kibbi mixture; pat and smooth over with wet hands. Use a sharp knife and cut into pieces.

Make a design all over the top using a fork. Spread melted butter over top.

Bake for 45-60 minutes, making sure it does not overcook.

Serve with yogurt and cucumber salad.

Fish

BBQ Salmon on Cedar Planks

2 cedar planks- soaked in water for 1 hour

1 kg salmon fillets

¼ cup olive oil

2 tsp salmon seasoning

½ cup butter, softened

¼ cup fresh dill, chopped

3 green onions, chopped

¼ tsp black pepper

juice of 2 limes

2 tsp salmon seasoning

slices of lemon and lime

dill weed

Spread olive oil all over the salmon; sprinkle 2 tsp of salmon seasoning over salmon. Set aside.

In a small bowl combine the remaining ingredients and mix well. Spread generously over salmon and place salmon on the cedar planks. Layer, decoratively, slices of lemon and lime and dill over the salmon. BBQ cedar planked salmon until salmon flakes easily with fork. Serve with tomato salsa and dilled rice.

Salsa for Fish

1 large onion, chopped

¼ cup olive oil

3 cloves garlic, minced

1 green pepper, chopped

2 - 19 oz cans diced tomatoes

¼ cup cilantro, chopped

½ tsp black pepper

salt to taste

2 tsp cumin

dash of cayenne pepper (optional)

1 tbsp vinegar

dash of cinnamon

¼ tsp seasoning salt

In a saucepan, on medium heat, add onion and olive oil. Cook until light brown; add remaining ingredients. Bring to a boil, reduce heat to low and simmer for 15 minutes. Serve with your favorite fish dish.

Stuffed Baked Fish

1 large whole fish, cleaned and seasoned with salt, pepper and drizzled with olive oil inside and out

Filling:

1 cup chopped parsley

½ cup chopped cilantro (optional)

4 cloves garlic, minced

1 - 2 jalapeño peppers, minced

1 green pepper, minced (optional)

¼ cup olive oil

¼ - ½ cup chopped walnuts

zest and juice of 2 lemons

1 tsp vinegar

1 tsp salt

1 tsp black pepper

2 tsp cajun seasoning or fish seasoning

dash of Tabasco sauce (optional)

Mix all of filling ingredients in a bowl; stuff fish with filling.

Place in a shallow roasting pan. Bake in 350°F oven uncovered 50 to 60 minutes or until fish flakes easily with fork.

(See picture at beginning of the chapter)

Fried Fish, Egyptian Style

This dressing may be used on a variety of fish, either whole fish or fillets.

fish of choice, cleaned

2 cups flour mixed with 2-3 tsp seasoning salt or fish seasoning

oil for frying

Sauce:

3 tsp cumin

1 tsp black pepper

½ cup olive oil

1 tsp seasoning salt

1 tbsp vinegar

1-2 tsp tabasco sauce

Combine ingredients in a bowl. Set aside.

Dip fish in sauce making sure to cover all of the fish. If using whole fish, be sure to coat the inside as well. Dip fish in flour mixture, shaking off excess. Heat oil and fry fish until golden.

Simple Fried Fish

1 kg fish – your choice

2 tsp salt

1 tsp pepper

½ cup vinegar

flour

olive oil – for deep frying

Clean fish, season with salt and pepper. Drizzle with vinegar and marinate for 20 minutes. Dip each piece of fish in flour and shake off excess.

Heat oil and fry fish until golden.

Deep-Fried Shrimp

1 kg uncooked large shrimp in shells, thawed if frozen
vegetable oil (for deep frying)
1 cup flour
2 tsp salt
1 tsp black pepper
4 large eggs
2 cups bread crumbs

Peel shrimp, leaving tails on. Make a shallow cut lengthwise down back of each shrimp and wash out vein.

Heat oil in a deep fryer.

In a bowl, mix flour, salt and pepper; set aside. In a second bowl, beat eggs and set aside. In a third bowl, place bread crumbs and set aside.

Coat shrimp in flour then dip into eggs and then coat with bread crumbs.

Fry shrimp, a few at a time in hot oil until golden brown. Place on a plate with paper towels in order to drain off excess oil after the cooking process is complete.

Shrimp in Tomato Sauce

1 kg uncooked medium shrimp, peeled and washed and deveined

¼ cup butter

¼ cup olive oil

1 large onion, chopped

1 large green pepper, chopped

1 cup celery, chopped

3 cloves garlic, minced

2 cups water

¼ cup parsley, chopped

2 tsp salt

¼ tsp cayenne pepper

2 bay leaves

2 - 14 oz cans tomato sauce

In a large pot, add and heat butter and olive oil over medium heat. Add onions, green peppers, celery and garlic and cook for 10 minutes, stirring occasionally until onions are tender. Stir in remaining ingredients except shrimp. Heat to boiling; reduce heat to low, simmer uncovered for 10 minutes.

Stir in Shrimp. Heat to boiling, reduce heat and cover. Cook 5- 10 minutes or until shrimp turns pink and firm. Remove bay leaves and serve over a hot bed of rice.

Lobster in White Sauce

¼ cup butter

3 tbsp flour

1 tsp salt

½ tsp ground mustard

½ tsp black pepper

2 cups milk

2 cups cooked lobster

3 tbsp apple juice

Melt butter in a saucepan over medium heat. Stir in flour, salt, mustard and pepper. Cook, stirring constantly, until smooth and bubbly; remove from heat. Stir in milk; bring to a boil, and stir constantly for 1 minute. Stir in lobster and apple juice. Heat through. Serve over rice.

Seafood Stew

½ lb uncooked medium shrimp, shelled and deveined

3 tbsp olive oil

1 cup carrots, thinly sliced

1 cup celery, sliced

1 cup onion, chopped

2 cloves garlic, finely chopped

1 - 14 oz can stewed or crushed tomatoes

2 cups water

2 beef bouillon cubes

1 cup potato, cut into ½ inch pieces

1 lb cod, cut into 1- inch pieces

1 - 14 oz can white or red beans

1 cup zucchini, sliced

1 tsp thyme

1 tsp black pepper

salt to taste

2 tbsp parsley, chopped

In a large pot, heat olive oil and add carrots, celery, onions, and garlic, stirring frequently, until vegetables are tender. Stir in tomatoes, water, bouillon and potatoes. Heat to boiling; reduce heat. Cover and simmer for 20 minutes, stirring occasionally. Stir in shrimp, cod, beans, zucchini, thyme, salt and pepper. Heat to boiling; reduce heat. Cover and simmer 10 minutes or until fish flakes easily with a fork and shrimp is pink and firm. Sprinkle with parsley.

Colourful Crab

Simple to make and very healthy too!

2 pkgs crab flakes (pollack flavoured)
2 cloves garlic, crushed
1 tbsp olive oil
1 green pepper, thinly sliced
1 red pepper, thinly sliced
2 onions, thinly sliced
seasoning salt, to taste

Heat olive oil in non- stick stir-fry pan on medium heat. Add garlic, sauté for one minute on low heat. Add crab flakes. Gently heat through until golden in colour. Add peppers, onions, and seasoning salt. Gently stir making sure not to over mix. Cook until vegetables are tender crisp.

Tuna Melts

2 slices bread, toasted
1 can flaked light tuna, packed in water
1 tsp pickle juice
1 tsp olive oil
cheddar cheese, sliced

In a bowl drain tuna, and add pickle juice and olive oil; mix.

Place toasted bread on cookie sheet. Lay bread flat and place tuna mixture on both pieces. Top with sliced cheese. Place cookie sheet in oven and broil until bubbly and golden. Enjoy while warm.

Bass Fish with Cilantro Sauce

2 bass fillets, medium sized, cleaned

½ tsp hot sauce

¼ cup red peppers, diced

1 tbsp garlic paste

¼ cup cilantro, fresh or dry, chopped

½ onion, chopped

½ tsp salt

¼ tsp pepper

½ lemon, squeezed

¼ cup almond slivers

1 tbsp olive oil

1 tbsp butter

2 tbsp water

Sauté almond slivers with butter until golden brown in saucepan, remove from heat and set aside.

In another saucepan sauté garlic, onion, and olive oil until onions are limp. Then add cilantro, red peppers, lemon juice, hot sauce, salt, pepper, and water. Simmer at medium heat for 5 minutes.

Place fillets on non-stick baking pan. Heat oven to 350ºF. Bake for 20 minutes until fish flakes. Place on a serving tray; add cilantro sauce to baked fish and sprinkle almond slivers over sauce and enjoy.

Basic Bread Dough

This basic bread dough is versatile enough to be used in a variety of recipes. It is most commonly used in savory pies and it can also be used for your pizza crust. This dough recipe is light and easy to work with.

4 cups flour

5 tbsp milk powder

1 tsp salt

3 tbsp sugar

2 tbsp instant quick rise yeast

½ cup vegetable oil

3 cups warm water

Mix the flour, milk powder, salt, sugar, and yeast in a large bowl. Make a well in the center of the flour mixture and add the oil and water to the flour mixture. Mix using your hands until the mixture comes together and the flour is well incorporated. If you find that the mixture is too sticky then add more flour, it depends on the brand of flour that you are using.

Add a ¼ cup at a time to the mixture until the flour is no longer sticking to the sides. Knead the dough for a good 5 minutes.

Add a tablespoon of oil and rub it on the dough as you form it into a ball.

Cover the dough with plastic wrap and place a tea towel over it. Keep the dough in a warm place and let it rise. When the dough has doubled in size, it is ready to use.

Tip

When baking, it is best to use light colored baking sheets (shiny silver colored baking sheets) instead of the nonstick baking sheets because the nonstick baking sheets are darker in color therefore they absorb a lot of the heat and can burn quickly. If you are using nonstick pans then reduce the heat of your oven temperature by 25° on any given recipe.

Feta Cheese Pies

These cheese pies are delicious. You can serve them warm or cold. To help speed things up, make the basic bread dough first before you make the filling.

1 Basic Bread Dough recipe (page 130)
4 cups chopped feta cheese
¼ cup finely chopped onion
¼ cup finely chopped parsley
1 cup shredded mozzarella cheese
3 tbsp melted butter
¼ cup olive oil
2 tsp sumac
½ tsp cayenne pepper
½ tsp black pepper
½ tsp oregano
½ tsp thyme

Preheat your oven to 450°F. Lightly grease a baking sheet. Set aside.

Cut the basic bread dough into golf ball size pieces. Form each piece into a ball and roll in flour. Arrange the pieces on a well floured surface and cover with plastic wrap. Then cover the formed balls with a tea towel. Remember to keep the dough balls a few inches away from each other so that they do not stick to each other.

In a large bowl, mix the feta cheese, mozzarella cheese, onion, and parsley. Add the butter, olive oil, sumac, cayenne pepper, black pepper, oregano and thyme. Mix together and set aside.

On a floured surface, take a dough ball and roll out to form a circle. You may use a rolling pin or your hands to form the circle. Once you have formed a circle, place a tablespoon of the filling in the center of the circle. Crimp the edges of the circle by pinching the dough all the way around the filling. Be creative and form various shapes, open triangles, squares or circles.

Place on prepared baking sheet as you continue to make more to fill the baking sheet. Keep the pieces about an inch apart. Bake until golden brown. Remove and cool on a wire rack; Store in a covered container.

Enjoy!

Tangy Spinach Pies

Fresh, lemony and good for you, spinach pies are irresistible.

1 Basic Bread Dough recipe (page 130)

4 packages frozen, chopped spinach (thawed)

½ cup finely chopped onion

1 cup chopped feta cheese

½ cup olive oil

juice of 2 lemons

1 tbsp sumac

2 tsp salt

1 tsp black pepper

½ tsp cayenne pepper

½ tsp thyme

½ tsp oregano (optional)

Preheat your oven to 450°F. Lightly grease a baking sheet. Set aside.

Cut the basic bread dough into golf ball size pieces or smaller if you desire. Form each piece into a ball and roll in flour. Arrange the pieces on a well floured surface and cover with plastic wrap. Then cover the formed balls with a tea towel. Remember to keep the dough balls a few inches away from each other so that they do not stick to each other.

Open the thawed spinach packages and squeeze out the liquid from the spinach, place in a large bowl. Add the onion, feta cheese, olive oil, lemon juice, sumac, salt, black pepper, cayenne pepper, thyme and oregano. Mix well and set aside.

On a floured surface, take a dough ball and roll out to form a circle. You may use a rolling pin or your hands to form the circle. Once you have formed a circle, place a tablespoon of the filling in the center of the circle. Fold the sides together and pinch to form a triangle. Place on prepared baking sheet about an inch apart. Bake until golden brown. Remove and cool on a wire rack; Store in a covered container.

Tip

When forming the spinach pies, be sure to keep the edges of the formed dough circle dry.
By keeping the edges dry, the dough will stick better and resist opening during baking.

Irresistible Meat Pies

Ground beef in a blend of spices make these pies a common favorite.

1 Basic Bread Dough recipe (page 130)

1 kg lean ground beef

2 ripe tomatoes peeled and finely diced

½ cup tomato sauce

¼ cup finely diced green pepper

½ cup finely diced onion

¼ cup finely chopped parsley

2 tbsp dry mint or ¼ cup fresh finely chopped mint

½ cup olive oil

2 tbsp salt

1 tsp black pepper

2 tsp steak spice (Montreal Steak Spice)

1 tbsp Worchestershire sauce

2 tsp all spice

¼ tsp ground cinnamon

¼ tsp cayenne pepper (optional)

Preheat your oven to 450°F. Lightly grease a baking sheet. Set aside.

Cut the basic bread dough into golf ball size pieces or smaller if you desire. Form each piece into a ball and roll in flour. Arrange the pieces on a well floured surface and cover with plastic wrap. Then cover the formed balls with a tea towel. Remember to keep the dough balls a few inches away from each other so that they do not stick to each other.

Place the ground beef in a large bowl. Add the remainder of the ingredients (except dough) and mix well until blended. Set aside.

On a floured surface, take a dough ball and roll out to form a circle. You may use a rolling pin or your hands to form the circle. Once you have formed a circle, place a tablespoon of the filling in the center of the circle. Fold the sides together and pinch to form a square or crimp the edges up around the filling to form an open circle. Place on prepared baking sheet about an inch apart. Bake until golden brown. Remove and cool on a wire rack; Store in a covered container.

Enjoy!

Saudi Style Meat Pies

These are served for Iftar (breaking of the fast) during the Holy Month of Ramadan. Traditionally, Samosa dough is used which can be purchased in your local grocery store.

1 kg ground beef or lamb

2 tsp turmeric powder

1 tsp black pepper powder

2 tsp salt or to taste

1½ tsp cumin powder

½ tsp coriander powder

2 cups finely chopped onion

¼ cup olive oil

1 cup finely chopped fresh mint

2 cups finely chopped celery leaves

2 cups finely chopped parsley

2 packages Samosa dough or 1 Basic Bread Dough recipe (page 130)

enough oil for frying (optional)

If you are using prepared Samosa dough, make sure to follow the instructions on the package and allow it to thaw before use.

In a large skillet or stock pot add the chopped onions and olive oil. Cook until wilted. Add the ground beef and brown. Add the mint, celery leaves, and parsley; stir then add turmeric, black pepper, salt, cumin, and coriander. Taste and adjust seasoning to your liking. If you like it spicy you may add a dash of cayenne pepper or finely diced hot pepper to the mixture. Set aside.

Take one sheet of Samosa dough and place a heaping spoonful of the meat mixture on one end of the sheet. Fold dough over the filling and alternate the folding to form a triangle seal the end making sure the filling is secure inside of the Samosa. Continue until all the Samosa sheets are used up. Heat enough oil in a deep fryer; add a few Samosas at a time, remove when golden brown. Drain on a platter lined with paper towels.

If you would like a healthier version, simply brush the Samosas with butter or oil and place on a baking sheet; bake in a 400°F oven until golden brown.

This filling may also be used with the Basic Bread dough Recipe. Simply prepare the basic bread dough as instructed and cut the basic bread dough into golf ball size pieces. Form each piece into a ball and roll in flour. Arrange the pieces on a well floured surface and cover with plastic wrap. Then cover the formed balls with a tea towel. Remember to keep the dough balls a few inches away from each other so that they do not stick to each other.

Prepare the Saudi Style meat pie filling and set aside.

On a floured surface, take a dough ball and roll out to form a circle. You may use a rolling pin or your hands to form the circle. Once you have formed a circle, place a tablespoon of the filling in the center of the circle. Fold the sides together and pinch to form a triangle. Place on prepared baking sheet about an inch apart. Bake until golden brown. Remove and cool on a wire rack; Store in a covered container.

Note

Celery leaves are commonly used in Saudi instead of the celery stalk it is called "Karafs" it is grown as a type of herb and the leaves are slightly larger than flat leaf parsley but if you prefer you may use finely chopped celery stalk but decrease the amount to ½ cup.

Potato Pies

These delicate, soft pies are a great comfort food. You can spice it up, make it a vegetarian dish or add ground beef for a hearty taste.

1 Basic Bread Dough recipe (page 130)

6 large potatoes –peeled and shredded

1 onion, diced fine

2 to 3 tomatoes, peeled and shredded

½ lb ground beef

1 tbsp dried mint

2 to 3 tsp salt

1 tsp black pepper

½ tsp cayenne pepper (optional)

½ cup peas (optional)

1 tbsp chicken or beef bouillon powder

½ tsp cinnamon

½ tsp cumin

½ tsp allspice

4 tbsp melted butter

Preheat your oven to 450°F. Lightly grease a baking sheet. Set aside.

Cut the basic bread dough into golf ball size pieces or smaller if you desire. Form each piece into a ball and roll in flour. Arrange the pieces on a well floured surface and cover with plastic wrap. Then cover the formed balls with a tea towel. Remember to keep the dough balls a few inches away from each other so that they do not stick to each other.

In a large skillet or pot, cook the onions in a few tablespoons of olive oil until limp. Add the ground beef and stir until cooked through (sprinkle a ¼ tsp of black pepper and ½ tsp seasoning salt over the meat). Add the shredded potatoes and cook until the potatoes are cooked half way through. Remove and pour the mixture into a large bowl. Add the remainder of the ingredients (except the dough) and mix well. At this point, you may want to taste the mixture to see if the desired level of spice and salt is adequate and to your liking. Set aside.

On a floured surface, take a dough ball and roll out to form a circle. You may use a rolling pin or your hands to form the circle. Once you have formed a circle, place a tablespoon of the filling in the center of the circle. Fold the sides together and pinch to form a triangle. Place on prepared baking sheet about an inch apart. Bake until golden brown. Remove and cool on a wire rack; Store in a covered container.

Variation – Omit the ground beef for a vegetarian style potato pie.

Tip

To keep the potatoes after shredding from turning red, soak the potatoes in cold water with a sprinkle of salt until they are ready to be used. Remember to squeeze out the excess water.

Mahamarah – Tomato Pies

Inspirational and fresh from the Mediterranean!

1 Basic Bread Dough recipe (page 130)

6 large, ripe tomatoes, peeled and chopped

½ cup fresh coriander, finely chopped

1 large onion, chopped

½ cup tomato sauce

¼ to ½ cup olive oil

1 roasted red bell pepper (remove the skin after roasting by scraping it off)

¼ cup walnuts, ground to a paste or use prepared walnut paste

2 tsp salt

1 tsp black pepper

½ tsp allspice

¼ tsp cinnamon

½ tsp red chili flakes (optional)

white cheddar cheese, thinly, sliced

Preheat your oven to 450°F. Lightly grease a baking sheet. Set aside.

Cut the basic bread dough into golf ball size pieces or larger if you desire. Form each piece into a ball and roll in flour. Arrange the pieces on a well floured surface and cover with plastic wrap. Then cover the formed balls with a tea towel. Remember to keep the dough balls a few inches away from each other so that they do not stick to each other once they rise.

Place all of the ingredients (except dough and cheese) into a food processor. Pulse the mixture until well blended. At this point, you may want to taste the mixture to see if the desired level of spice and salt is adequate and to your liking. Set aside.

On a floured surface, take a dough ball and roll it out to form a circle. You may use a rolling pin or your hands to form the circle. Once you have formed a circle, place it on the prepared baking sheet and then place 1 to 2 tablespoon of the filling in the center of the circle (depending on the size of the dough circle) and spread it all over the circle.

Place a few slices of the cheddar cheese on top. Repeat with the remainder of the dough.

Bake until golden brown. Remove and cool on a wire rack;

Store in a covered container.

Enjoy!

Tip

To peel tomatoes quickly, place the tomatoes in a large bowl and prick with a knife. Pour boiling water over the tomatoes and wait 5 minutes, drain. Pour cold water over the tomatoes, drain and peel.

Zaatar Pies

A blend of oregano, thyme, sumac and sometimes sesame seeds, this Mediterranean mix can be found in most supermarkets today. Excellent for breakfast!

½ **Basic Bread Dough recipe (page 130)**
1 **cup Zaatar**
½ **to ¾ cup extra virgin olive oil**

Preheat your oven to 450°F. Lightly grease a baking sheet. Set aside.

Cut the basic bread dough into golf ball size pieces or larger if you desire. Form each piece into a ball and roll in flour. Arrange the pieces on a well floured surface and cover with plastic wrap. Then cover the formed balls with a tea towel. Remember to keep the dough balls a few inches away from each other so that they do not stick to each other once they rise.

In a mixing bowl add the Zaatar and gradually add the olive oil until the mixture is slightly runny. Set aside.

On a floured surface, take a dough ball and roll it out to form a circle. You may use a rolling pin or your hands to form the circle. Once you have formed a circle, place it on the prepared baking sheet and then place 1 to 2 tablespoon of the filling in the center of the circle (depending on the size of the dough circle) use your fingers to make indentation marks all over the dough as you spread the mixture to cover the dough circle.

Repeat with the remainder of the dough. Bake until the bottom of each circle is light brown. Remove and cool on a wire rack; Store in a covered container. Enjoy!

Pizza

3½ cups flour (about 1 lb)
1½ cups warm water (about 10oz)
1 tsp active dry yeast
1 tbsp olive oil
1 tbsp salt

PIZZA SAUCE
1 - 14 oz can crushed tomato
3 tbsp oregano
1 tbsp thyme
2 cloves garlic, crushed
1 tsp black pepper
2 tsp salt
1-2 tsp sugar

Mix all ingredients for the pizza sauce in a bowl and set aside.

Place flour in a large bowl; make a well in the center of the flour. Pour warm water in the center of the flour. Add yeast to the warm water. Stir the warm water and yeast gently, do not mix in the flour just yet; set aside to allow the yeast to froth about 3 minutes. Add olive oil and salt to the yeast; stir, gently fold in flour from the sides. Remove dough onto a floured work surface and knead for 10 minutes. Form dough into a ball and place into a greased bowl. Cover with plastic wrap and a tea towel. Allow to rise until double, about 2 - 3 hours.

Punch down dough and cut into 3 equal portions. Roll each portion into a ball; cover and allow to rise a second time for another 20 minutes.

Roll each portion into a circle. Place on a greased pizza pan. Spread a few tablespoons of pizza sauce over the dough. Add your favourite meat and vegetable toppings, sprinkle with shredded mozzarella cheese and bake in a 500°F oven until cheese is melted and edges are golden brown.

Roti

A simple and quick bread to make

2 cups whole wheat flour
1 tsp salt
1 tsp melted butter or ghee
enough lukewarm water to form dough

Place the flour and salt in a food processor. Add salt and butter. Mix; Start food processor and add warm water until the mixture forms a dough.

Remove dough and knead together. Divide dough into equal golf size portions. Cover with a clean tea towel or plastic wrap.

Preheat a nonstick skillet on medium high heat. Form each portion of dough into rounds. Place the round in the skillet and cook for approximately a minute or until light brown patches/spots appear. Flip and cook the other side of the Roti. Place on a plate and cover with a clean tea towel. Continue with the remainder of the dough. Stack each roti on top of one another as each one is done and cover with a clean tea towel to prevent from drying out.

To store, when the Rotis are cool, place in a storage bag and refrigerate. When ready to eat, heat and serve.

Note

You may purchase roti makers or specially made roti skillets from specialty stores.

Iranian Bread or Tanoor Bread

This bread is traditionally baked in upright clay ovens called "Tanoor"
This bread is very popular in the Gulf Region. Delicious!

6 cups brown flour or (3 cups white flour and 3 cups brown flour)
1½ tsp active dry yeast
1 tsp sugar
2 to 3 cups lukewarm water

Dissolve the yeast and sugar in ¼ cup of warm water. Set aside to proof. In a large bowl add the flour and salt; make a well in the center. Pour in the dissolved yeast mixture. Gradually add warm water while mixing by hand until soft dough is formed. Knead on a floured surface for 10 to 15 minutes until smooth and elastic. Form into a ball and place in a greased bowl. Turn greased side up and cover with plastic wrap and a clean tea towel. Place in a warm place and allow to rest for 30 minutes. Knead the dough again and form into a ball. Allow to rest for another 45 minutes or until double.

Divide the dough into small balls about the size of a tennis ball. Roll in flour and set aside. Cover with plastic wrap and a clean tea towel.

Preheat the oven to 400°F. Place an oven tray or cookie tray in the oven and heat it for 3 minutes. Meanwhile, rollout each dough ball into a 30 cm diameter circle on floured work surface. Prick the dough and slide it onto the preheated oven tray. Bake until golden. Cover the bread as soon as it is cool to prevent it from drying out; Store in storage bags.

This bread freezes well. To reheat sprinkle a little water over the bread and heat in the oven or microwave for 30 seconds. Serve warm.

Variation

Sesame bread- Sprinkle sesame seeds on the bread before baking.

Skillet Meat Pockets

DOUGH

4 cups flour

4 tbsp powdered milk

3 tbsp softened butter

1 tsp sugar

½ tsp yeast

1 tsp salt

½ tsp baking powder

1½ cups warm water

FILLING

2 cups ground beef

1 cup chopped onion

1 tsp minced garlic

¼ cup chopped dill

¼ cup toasted pine nuts

1 tsp salt or to taste

1 tsp ground black pepper

1 tsp turmeric

2 tbsp butter

To prepare the dough, in a large bowl mix the dry dough ingredients. Make a well in the center and add the softened butter and warm water. Knead until smooth about 5 to 10 minutes. Form into a ball and place into a greased bowl. Turn the dough greased side up. Cover in plastic wrap and a tea towel. Let rise until double in size about one hour.

To prepare filling, place meat in a large skillet and cook until browned and excess liquid produced from the meat has evaporated. Add the butter, onion, garlic and dill; season with salt, black pepper, and turmeric. Cook for a few minutes; add 1 cup of water and simmer until water has evaporated. Add pine nuts and mix well. Set aside.

Divide the dough into small balls and roll each piece into a flat circle. Fill half of the formed dough rounds with a tablespoon of the meat filling. Place another dough round on top of each filled round and seal edges.

In a skillet, fry the dough rounds in a little bit of oil until golden on both sides.

Vegetable Stuffed Pockets

DOUGH

4 cups flour

½ cup mashed potato

2 tbsp oil

1 tbsp baking powder

1 tsp salt

1 tbsp sugar

1¼ cups water

oil for deep frying

FILLING

1 cup chopped carrots

1 cup chopped onion

1 cup chopped cabbage

1 cup bean sprouts

¼ cup chopped coriander

3 tbsp melted butter

1 tsp salt or to taste

1 tsp black pepper

splash of soya sauce

To prepare the dough, in a large bowl sift dry dough ingredients; add the mashed potato, water and 2 tbsp of oil to the dry ingredients. Knead well, about 5 minutes. Form dough into a ball, cover and place in a warm place until double in size, about 1 hour.

For the filling, in a large skillet add onions and butter; cook until onions are wilted; add remaining filling ingredients and cook until vegetables are tender. Set aside.

To assemble; Divide dough into small equal balls. Roll each piece into a flat circle. Fill each circle with 1 tablespoon of the vegetable filling. Fold each circle in half to form a semi-circle, pinch the edges firmly together. Deep Fry in hot oil until golden brown.

> Variation
> Instead of frying, bake at 350°F until golden brown.

Urban

Special lightly sweetened bread. Bakers can be found plentifully baking this type of bread in Lebanon.

2 cups sugar

2 cups warm water

2 cups warm milk

2 tbsp flower water or rose water

2 tbsp ground mahleb (available in Middle Eastern stores)

3 tbsp dry active yeast

1 tsp baking powder

7 to 9 cups flour

GLAZE

½ cup icing sugar

¼ cup rose water or flower water (optional)

In a large bowl, mix the sugar, warm water, warm milk, flower water, mahleb and yeast. Add one cup of flour and baking powder, stir and mix. Add the remainder of the flour one cup at a time until it forms a soft dough. Knead until smooth and elastic and no longer sticky, adding more flour if necessary. Form into a ball and place in a greased bowl. Turn greased side up and cover with plastic wrap and a tea towel. Place in a warm place and allow to double in size. Punch the dough down and form into a ball again. Cover and allow to rest until double in size again.

Divide dough into equal portions and form into balls. Flatten each ball into a round about an inch thick. Place on a floured and greased baking sheet. Cover again with plastic wrap and tea towel; allow to rest for 15 minutes. Remove plastic wrap and tea towel. Preheat oven 400°F and bake until golden brown.

If desired, in a small bowl, mix ½ cup icing sugar and ¼ cup flower water or rose water; using a pastry brush, spread mixture lightly over each loaf. If you prefer you may omit the icing sugar and brush each loaf with the flower water or rose water instead.

Variation

Place 2 cups of pitted dates into a cooking pot; add ¼ cup of milk and cook over medium heat. Transfer the mixture to a food processor and blend until smooth; set aside.

Roll out a quarter of the dough into a rectangle and place a strip of the filling on the widest end. Roll jelly style roll; pinch ends. Coil into a disk allow to rest and bake as directed. Vary the size by using less or more of the dough.

Lebanese Bread

This bread is very versatile and can be used to make zaatar pies, cheese pies, open faced meat pies, pizza or plain flat bread. Be creative and use this dough as your canvas and top it with your own creation.

2 ½ tbsp active dry yeast

2 ½ cups warm water or more if needed

1 tbsp sugar

2 tsp salt

8 cups flour

4 tbsp vegetable oil

Dissolve the yeast in a ¼ cup of warm water, add sugar and set aside for 10 to 15 minutes.

Mix the flour and salt in a large bowl and place in a warm oven for a few minutes to warm slightly. Pour the yeast mixture into a well in the center of the flour and mix by hand, adding the warm water gradually. Knead well to form soft dough. Turn the dough out onto a lightly floured work surface and knead for 15 to 20 minutes. Knead in the oil and form a ball. Place in a greased bowl and turn the dough greased side up. Cover with plastic wrap and a tea towel. Place in a warm place to rise until double in size, about 1 to 2 hours. Preheat the oven to maximum heat.

Punch the dough down and reform the ball. Turn out onto a floured work surface and knead for 2 minutes. Divide the dough into 8 equal pieces and roll out each piece into a ball. Form and roll each piece into a round flat shape about a ¼ inch thick. Place the dough rounds onto a floured surface and cover with plastic wrap and a tea towel; allow to rest for 30 minutes.

Place a baking sheet in the heated oven for 5 minutes, remove and lightly grease with oil; place a dough round onto the greased baking sheet and bake 4 to 8 minutes or until lightly browned. Continue with the remainder of the dough. Cool and store in a sealed container.

Middle Eastern Cheese Bread

4 cups flour

2 cups akawi cheese, shredded

3 tbsp sugar

½ cup chopped parsley

1 tsp dried or fresh chopped mint

1 tsp oregano

¼ cup vegetable oil

1 tbsp instant dry yeast

1 cup water

In a large bowl combine cheese and all dry ingredients and mix well. Add water and oil; mix and knead well until a smooth dough forms about 5 minutes. Form dough into a ball, cover with plastic wrap and a clean tea towel. Allow to rest in a warm place for 1 hour or until double in size.

Preheat oven to 400°F.

Divide dough into equal portions. Roll out each portion into a circle about ¼ to ½ inch thickness. Arrange on a greased baking sheet. Bake until golden brown. Remove from pan, cool and store in an airtight container or bag.

Variation

You may substitute any type of cheese for the akawi cheese.

Corn Bread Muffins

3 cups cornmeal

1 cup flour

½ cup vegetable oil or shortening

3 cups buttermilk

4 tsp baking powder

2 tsp sugar

2 tsp salt

1 tsp baking soda

4 eggs

½ cup corn niblets

Preheat oven to 450°F. Grease the bottoms only of muffin pans. Set aside.

Mix all the ingredients in a large bowl and beat well. Fill muffin tins ¾ full. Bake for 20 minutes or when a toothpick inserted in center comes out clean.

Note

If you do not have muffin tins, you may use two 8 x 8 x 2 inch square pans. Make sure to grease the pan before pouring in the corn bread mixture. Bake for 25 to 30 minutes or until golden brown.

Baking Powder Biscuits

The secret to light and fluffy biscuits is to make sure not to over knead the dough.
Treat this dough gently and you will be rewarded.

2 cups flour or whole wheat flour
½ cup shortening
1 tbsp sugar
3 tsp baking powder
1 tsp salt
¾ cup milk

Preheat oven to 450°F. In a large bowl, mix flour, sugar, baking powder and salt. Add the shortening and mix with a pastry blender until mixture resembles fine crumbs. Stir in just enough milk until mixture forms a ball. The dough should not be too sticky or too dry. Turn dough out onto a work surface and knead lightly for 30 seconds. Roll dough out to ½ inch thick. Use a floured biscuit cutter and cut out biscuits. Place on an ungreased cookie sheet about 1 inch apart for crusty sides or touching for soft sides. Bake 12 minutes or until golden brown. Remove from cookie sheet and let cool.

Variation

For Buttermilk Biscuits – decrease the baking powder to 2 teaspoons and add ¼ tsp baking soda with the salt. Substitute buttermilk for the milk.

Delicate Tender Biscuits

1½ tbsp instant yeast

2 tbsp warm water

1 cup shortening

5 cups flour

¼ cup sugar

3 tsp baking powder

2 tsp salt

1 tsp baking soda

2 cups buttermilk

Dissolve the yeast in warm water; Set aside.

In a large bowl mix flour, sugar, baking powder, salt and baking soda; add the shortening and mix with a pastry blender until mixture resembles fine crumbs. Stir in yeast mixture and buttermilk. The dough will be soft and sticky.

Turn the dough out onto a floured surface. Knead lightly 20 to 30 times. If dough is too sticky, sprinkle lightly with flour. Roll out ½ inch thick. Cut with round cutter. Place on an ungreased cookie sheet 1 inch apart. Cover and let rise in a warm place for 1 hour or until double.

Heat oven to 400°F. Bake for 12 minutes or until golden brown.

Basic Scones

Try these scones with cream cheese or butter and jam, Yum!!

½ cup butter

2 cups flour

3 tbsp sugar

2 ½ tsp baking powder

¼ tsp salt

1 beaten egg

½ cup raisins or dried fruit (optional)

6 to 8 tbsp half-and-half cream

1 egg, beaten

Preheat oven to 400°F. In a large bowl mix flour, sugar, baking powder and salt. Add butter and mix with a pastry blender until mixture resembles fine crumbs. Stir in 1 egg and raisins (or dried fruit) and just enough half-and-half until dough leaves the side of bowl.

Turn dough out onto floured surface. Knead dough a few times. Roll out ½ inch thick. Cut with a floured biscuit cutter or cut into triangles. Place on ungreased cookie sheet. Brush dough with beaten egg. Bake 12 minutes or until golden brown.

Variations

For a cheesy scone, omit the dried fruit and add ½ cup of your favorite shredded cheese.
For a fruit scone, add 1 tsp cinnamon or nutmeg with the salt.
Substitute ½ cup of dried blueberries or cranberries for the raisins.

Pancakes

You can personalize your pancakes in various ways. Try adding fresh berries or bananas to the batter or chocolate chips. Get creative!

2 eggs

2 cups flour

2 cups milk (more if you like your pancakes slightly thinner)

2 tbsp sugar or brown sugar

4 tbsp vegetable oil

6 tsp baking powder

½ tsp salt

In a large bowl, beat eggs with mixer until light and fluffy, 3 to 4 minutes. Beat in remaining ingredients until smooth. Heat skillet or griddle over medium heat. Grease skillet and pour ¼ cup of batter onto hot skillet. Cook pancakes until dry around the edges and brown at the bottom. Flip and cook the other side. Continue with remaining batter.

French Toast

This is a great recipe for using up your stale bread. Tastes Great!

½ cup flour

1½ cups milk

2 tbsp sugar

1 tsp vanilla

¼ tsp salt

6 eggs

½ tsp cinnamon or nutmeg (optional)

15 slices bread

In a large bowl, beat flour, milk, sugar, vanilla, salt and eggs until smooth. Heat griddle or skillet over medium heat. Grease skillet. Dip bread into egg mixture. Cook about 3 to 4 minutes on each side or until golden brown. Serve with maple syrup, pancake syrup or a dusting of icing sugar and fruit slices on the side.

Variation

To make overnight Custard French toast, Prepare as directed but layer the bread in a baking dish and pour the egg mixture over the bread. Turn the bread to coat the other side. Cover and refrigerate overnight. Cook as directed but increase the cooking time to 6 minutes per side or until golden brown.

Banana Bread

This is an all time favorite, very moist and cake like. This bread freezes well. Try it with vanilla or maple walnut ice cream for a great quick dessert. Enjoy!

2 ½ cups sugar

1 cup butter

4 eggs

3 cups mashed ripe bananas

1 cup buttermilk

2 tsp vanilla

5 cups flour

2 tsp baking soda

2 tsp salt

1 cup walnuts (optional)

½ cup mini chocolate chips (optional)

Preheat oven to 350°F. Grease the bottoms only of 2 large loaf pans. Set aside.

In a large bowl, mix sugar and butter until fluffy. Stir in eggs until well blended. Add bananas, buttermilk and vanilla. Beat until smooth. Stir in flour, baking soda and salt until moistened, do not over beat. Stir in nuts and chocolate chips if desired. Pour into greased pans. Bake about 1 hour or until toothpick inserted in center comes out clean. Cool for 10 minutes. Remove from pans and cool completely before slicing.

Cinnamon Sticky Buns

Soft, fragrant and delicious!!

DOUGH

4 cups flour

⅓ cup sugar

1 tsp salt

2 tbsp active or instant dry yeast

1 cup warm milk

⅓ cup butter, softened

1 egg

FILLING

1 cup packed brown sugar

¼ cup sugar

½ cup softened butter

2 tsp cinnamon

½ tsp nutmeg

½ cup chopped pecans or walnuts (optional)
or ½ cup raisins (optional)

To prepare the dough: Mix 2 cups of flour, sugar, salt and yeast in a large bowl. Add warm milk, butter, and egg. Beat on low speed for 1 minute, scraping bowl frequently. Stir in enough remaining flour until dough is easy to handle. Turn dough out onto floured surface and knead for 5 minutes. Place in a greased bowl and turn greased side up. Cover with plastic wrap and a clean tea towel. Place in a warm place for one hour or until double in size.

Prepare the filling by mixing all filling ingredients except the nuts or raisins. Set aside.

Punch down dough and flatten with hands. Using a rolling pin, rollout into a large rectangle about a ¼ inch thick. Spread the filling over the dough. Leave the ends of the dough without filling, by doing this the dough will be easier to seal. Sprinkle the nuts or raisins over the filling if desired.

Start with the longest side of the rectangular shaped dough by rolling the dough tightly into a jelly roll style. Seal the edges by pinching the ends together. Stretch and shape until even. Use a knife and score lightly over the rolled dough to mark even 1 inch slices. For easy slicing, use a strong piece of sewing thread and place underneath the dough. Lift the ends of the thread and crisscross to cut the dough easily into pieces. If you do not have thread, use a sharp knife to cut the pieces evenly. Use the marks you have made as a guide to cut even pieces. Place each piece on a greased baking sheet. Cover and let rise in a warm place for 30 minutes or until double.

Heat the oven to 350°F. Bake for 30 minutes or until golden brown. Immediately invert onto a serving tray or heat proof tray allowing the filling to drizzle down.

Traditional Rolls

This recipe is very versatile. The dough can be used to make various shapes of rolls, all with ease.

4 cups flour

¼ cup sugar

¼ cup shortening or butter, softened

1 tsp salt

2 tbsp instant yeast

½ cup very warm water

½ cup very warm milk

1 egg

butter softened for brushing

In a large bowl, mix 2 cups of flour, sugar, shortening, salt and yeast. Make a well in the center and add warm water, warm milk, and egg. Beat on low speed for 1 minute. Beat on medium speed for 1 minute. Stir in enough of the remaining flour to make the dough easy to handle. Turn the dough out onto a floured work surface. Knead for 5 minutes. Place in a greased bowl and turn greased side up. Cover with plastic wrap and a clean tea towel. Let rise in a warm place for about an hour or until double.

Punch down dough and cut into equal size pieces. Shape into balls. Place close together in a greased pan. Brush with butter and cover. Let rise about 30 minutes or until double.

Heat oven to 400°F. Bake for 12 to 15 minutes or until golden brown.

Shape variations

Cloverleaf rolls – Cut dough into 36 pieces. Shape into balls. Place 3 balls in each of 12 greased muffin cups. Continue as directed above.

Crescent rolls – Roll out half of dough into a large circle. Spread butter over circle. Cut circle into wedges. Roll each wedge, beginning at rounded edge, to form a crescent. Place each crescent onto a greased baking sheet with the point down. Continue with the remainder of dough and as directed above.

Danish Pastries

These are worth the effort and time to make.

2 tbsp active dry yeast

½ cup warm water

1 tsp sugar

4 cups flour

⅓ cup sugar

2 tsp salt

1 cup cold butter, cut into small pieces

4 eggs

1 cup milk

jam or preserves

powdered sugar glaze
(see recipe below)

For the Danish, in a large bowl, add 1 tsp sugar and warm water. Add the yeast and set aside. Wait a few minutes to allow the mixture to proof. Add in the flour, sugar and salt. Cut in the butter with a pastry blender until mixture resembles fine crumbs. Separate the eggs and refrigerate egg whites for later use. Stir the egg yolks and milk into the flour mixture until soft dough forms. Shape into a ball and cover bowl with plastic wrap. Refrigerate for 8 hours or overnight.

Punch dough down and divide into 3 equal parts. Work with one part at a time while keeping the remainder of the dough in the refrigerator.

On a floured surface, roll out one part of dough into a rectangle. Cut into 1 inch strips. Take each strip and pinch the ends together to form a ring. Twist to form a figure 8. Place on a greased cookie sheet, two inches apart. Brush with egg white. Let rise uncovered for 25 minutes.

Heat oven to 350°F. Make an indentation in the center of each loop and fill with a teaspoon of jam or preserves. Brush dough with egg white. Bake for 15 minutes or until golden brown. Cool and drizzle with glaze.

Powdered Sugar Glaze

1½ cups powdered sugar

1 tsp vanilla

2 to 3 tbsp milk

Mix all ingredients until smooth. If needed add a little more milk, a teaspoon at a time to reach desired consistency.

Cheesy Garlic Bread

You may use French bread or any type of crusty bread. Great with any pasta dish.

½ cup butter, softened
1 garlic clove, crushed
½ tsp dry oregano
2 tsp chopped fresh parsley
3 tbsp grated Parmesan cheese
1 cup mozzarella cheese, shredded
1 loaf French bread or any large crusty bread

Preheat oven to 400°F. In a bowl, mix butter, crushed garlic, oregano, parsley and Parmesan cheese; Set aside. Cut bread into equal slices and place on a baking sheet. Spread the butter mixture over each slice. Sprinkle the mozzarella cheese over each slice. Bake in oven until edges are golden and cheese is bubbly.

Note

For a quick version, follow the instructions above but place the tray of garlic bread under a broiler and watch carefully until light golden brown.

Desserts

1 Baklava (page 197)

2 Cream of Wheat Squares (page 201)

3 Date Filled Cookies (page 207)

4 Ma'amoul (page 199)

5 Macaroni Pastries (page 203)

6 Cherry Cups (page 196)

7 Carrot Cake (page 183)

8 Brownies (page 169)

9 Jam Squares (page 173)

10 Date Squares (page 175)

11 Pecan Tarts (page 192)

Chocolate Chip Cookies

The ultimate chocolate experience!

1 cup butter or margarine

¾ cup brown sugar, packed

½ cup sugar

1 large egg

1 tsp vanilla

2 ½ cups flour

1 tsp baking soda

1 tsp cinnamon

2 cups chocolate chips

Preheat oven to 375°F.

Mix butter, brown sugar, and sugar in a large bowl using an electric mixer. Add egg and vanilla and beat well.

In another bowl add flour, baking soda, and cinnamon. Mix well. Add dry ingredients to the creamed mixture. Mix well. Stir in chocolate chips.

Roll into 2-inch balls (about two tablespoons). Flatten slightly with fork about two inches apart onto cookie sheet.

Bake for approximately 9-11 minutes or until lightly browned. Let cool for 5 minutes, then remove to a tightly sealed container to keep the cookies soft and chewy. Makes approximately 20 cookies.

Chocolate Chip Nut Cookies

This recipe is perfect for a large crowd!

2 cups butter, softened

2 cups brown sugar, packed

1⅓ cups sugar

4 large eggs

4 tsp vanilla

5 cups flour

2 tsp baking soda

1 tsp salt

3 cups chocolate chips

1 cup walnuts or pecans, chopped

Preheat oven to 375°F.

Mix butter, brown sugar, and sugar in a large bowl using an electric mixer. Add eggs and vanilla and beat well.

In another bowl add flour, baking soda, and salt. Mix well. Add dry ingredients to the creamed mixture. Mix well. Stir in chocolate chips and chopped nuts.

Drop cookie dough by tablespoonfuls onto an ungreased cookie sheet about two inches apart.

Bake for approximately 9-11 minutes or until lightly browned. Let cool for 1 minute, and then remove to a cooling rack. Once cool, store in an airtight container to keep the cookies soft and chewy.

Oatmeal Chocolate Chip Cookies

So yummy and chewy!

1¼ cups butter or margarine (room temperature)

¾ cup brown sugar

½ cup sugar

1 large egg

1 tsp vanilla

2 ½ cups flour

1 tsp baking soda

½ tsp salt

1 tsp cinnamon

⅛ tsp nutmeg

3 cups quick rolled oats

1 cup chocolate chips

½ cup walnuts, chopped (optional)

Preheat oven to 350° F.

Cream butter, brown sugar, and sugar in a large bowl. Beat in egg and vanilla using an electric mixer. Beat well.

In another bowl stir flour, baking soda, salt, cinnamon and nutmeg. Add to creamed mixture, stirring well. Mix in oats, chocolate chips and walnuts.

Drop dough by tablespoonfuls about 2 inches apart onto cookie sheet. Bake for approximately 9-11 minutes or until golden. Makes 30 cookies.

Oatmeal Raisin Cookies: Substitute 1 cup raisins for chocolate chips

Double Chocolate Chip Cookies

What a delectable treat, especially warm!

1 cup butter or margarine, softened

¾ cup brown sugar

½ cup sugar

1 large egg

1 tsp vanilla

1¾ cups flour

⅓ cup cocoa

1 tsp baking soda

½ tsp salt

2 cups chocolate chips

1 cup pecans or walnuts, chopped

Preheat oven to 375°F.

Cream butter, brown sugar, and sugar in a large bowl. Beat in egg and vanilla with mixer, mixing well.

In another bowl mix flour, cocoa, baking soda and salt. Add to creamed mixture and blend well. Add in chocolate chips and nuts.

Drop by teaspoons about two inches apart onto a cookie sheet and bake for 9-11 minutes. Let cool and store in sealed container to keep cookies chewy. Makes about two-dozen cookies.

> Variation
>
> Instead of 2 cups of chocolate chips, substitute 1 cup white chocolate chips and 1 cup chocolate chips and omit nuts.

Hermits

A nutty and chewy delight!

2 cups flour

½ tsp salt

1 tsp baking powder

¼ tsp nutmeg

¼ tsp allspice

½ cup butter or margarine

2 eggs

1 tsp vanilla

½ cup raisins

½ cup walnuts, chopped

½ cup dates, chopped

Preheat oven to 350°F.

In a small mixing bowl mix flour, salt, baking powder, nutmeg and allspice. Set aside.

Cream butter and sugar together. Beat in eggs and vanilla using an electric hand mixer. Add in dry ingredients, and then add in raisins, walnuts, and dates. Mix well.

Drop by teaspoons about two inches apart onto a cookie sheet and bake for 15-18 minutes.

Banana Drops

Great way to use up leftover bananas!

2 tsp baking powder

¼ tsp baking soda

1 tsp cinnamon

2 ¼ cups flour

⅔ cup butter, softened

1 cup sugar

2 eggs

1 cup bananas, mashed

1 tsp vanilla

Preheat oven to 400°F.

In a small mixing bowl mix baking powder, baking soda, cinnamon and flour, set aside. In a large bowl cream butter and sugar. Beat in eggs, mashed bananas, and vanilla, beating well with a mixer. Stir in dry ingredients and blend well.

Drop by tablespoonfuls onto a cookie sheet placing them 3 inches apart.

Bake for about 10-15 minutes or until golden in colour. Makes about 2-dozen cookies.

Variation

This recipe can also be made into muffins or a cake.

Brownies

Bet you can't eat just one!

1⅓ cups flour
1 tsp baking powder
½ tsp salt
1 cup butter
2 cups sugar
1 cup cocoa
4 eggs
2 tsp vanilla
½ cup walnuts, chopped

Preheat oven to 350° F.

In a mixing bowl mix flour, baking powder, and salt. Set aside.

Melt butter in a saucepan. Let cool.

In a large bowl blend cooled butter and cocoa together. Beat in sugar, eggs and vanilla.

Add the flour mixture and blend well with a large spoon just until blended. Stir in walnuts.

Spread in 13 by 9 inch greased cake pan. Bake for about 30-35 minutes or until toothpick inserted in center comes out clean. Cool completely, then ice with chocolate icing. Cut into bars.

Chocolate Icing

3 cups icing sugar
¼ cup butter or margarine, softened
2 tsp vanilla
¼ cup cocoa
2 to 3 tbsp milk

Mix all ingredients except milk in a bowl. Stir in milk until smooth.

When adding milk, add a tablespoon at a time to see how much milk is needed.

Beat until smooth. This recipe can be used on any cake or cupcakes.

Marshmallow Rice Squares

6 cups puffed rice cereal
32 large marshmallows or 3 cups miniature marshmallows
¼ cup butter
1 tsp vanilla

In a large bowl add the puffed rice cereal; set aside.

Heat marshmallows and butter in a saucepan over low heat, stirring constantly, until marshmallows are melted and mixture is smooth.

Remove from heat and add vanilla; stir well.

Add mixture to the puffed rice cereal mix and coat evenly. Spread and press mixture evenly in a greased baking pan. Cool and cut into bars.

Puffed Wheat Squares

8 cups puffed wheat cereal
¾ cup corn syrup
¼ cup butter
¼ cup brown sugar
3 tbsp cocoa
1 tsp vanilla

In a large bowl measure out puffed wheat and set aside.

In a medium saucepan add corn syrup, butter, brown sugar, cocoa, and vanilla.

Let boil over low heat for one minute, remove from heat.

Pour mixture over puffed wheat and mix well. Pour and press into a greased 13 by 9 inch baking pan. Let cool and cut into squares.

Dream Bars

1½ cups flour

1 cup brown sugar

1 cup chopped pecans

6 tbsp unsalted butter, softened

3 eggs

1 tsp vanilla

½ tsp baking powder

¼ tsp salt

1½ cups unsweetened coconut flakes

1 (14 ounce) can sweetened condensed milk

Line a 13 by 9 inch baking pan with foil so that it covers the bottom and overhangs 2 sides by 1- inch. Tuck the overlap around the outside of the pan; coat with a non-stick baking spray.

Preheat the oven to 350°F.

In a bowl, combine 1 cup of the flour, ½ cup of the brown sugar, and the pecans. Mix with a pastry blender until the mixture resembles lumpy crumbs. Lightly pat the streusel mixture into the baking pan. Set aside.

In a mixing bowl, beat together the eggs and the remaining ½ cup brown sugar until doubled in volume. Beat in the vanilla. Set aside.

In another mixing bowl, sift together the remaining ½ cup flour, baking powder, and salt. Add this mixture to the egg mixture and mix well.

Pour mixture on top of the streusel in the baking pan.

Sprinkle on the coconut and the sweetened condensed milk.

Bake for 25 to 30 minutes. Cool; run a knife around the edges to loosen.

Using the foil in the pan, lift the bars out of the pan and cut into 2-inch bars.

Chocolate Squares

Delicious!!

CRUST:

1 cup butter, softened

2 eggs

2 tsp vanilla

2 cups brown sugar

2 ½ cups flour

1 tsp baking soda

1 tsp salt

3 cups rolled oats

CHOCOLATE FILLING:

2 cups semi-sweet chocolate chips

1 cup condensed milk

2 tsp butter

1 tsp vanilla

In a large bowl combine all the crust ingredients and mix together with your hands until crumbly. Place half of mixture into a 13 by 9 inch greased baking pan and press flat to cover the baking pan and set aside.

For the filling, in a saucepan add all the filling ingredients and melt on low heat. Remove from heat and spread over the oat mixture in the baking pan. Crumble the other half of the oat mixture over the chocolate filling making sure to cover all of the chocolate filling.

Bake in 350°F oven for 25 minutes or until golden brown. Cool and cut into squares; Store in an airtight container.

Variation for caramel-chocolate squares

In a saucepan add 64 caramel squares and 1 can of evaporated milk. On low heat, stir until caramels are melted. Remove from heat. Pour mixture over chocolate layer and continue with above recipe.

Jam Squares

A must-have with coffee and company!

1 cup butter or margarine, softened

1 cup sugar

2 eggs

1 tsp vanilla

3-3 ½ cups flour

1 tsp baking powder

½ jar jam, raspberry or apricot

Preheat oven to 350° F.

Cream butter and sugar in a large mixing bowl.

Beat in eggs and vanilla with an electric mixer. Beat until smooth.

Add in 3 cups flour and baking powder. Mix well with hands. Dough should be like pie dough. If you need more flour add a bit more.

Spread a bit more than half of dough in a 13 by 9 inch greased cake pan. By tablespoonfuls spread jam on the bottom layer. Spread evenly.

Take a grater (using the large holes) and grate the remainder of dough evenly over the jam layer. Bake for approximately 30 minutes or until the top is golden in colour. Let cool and cut into squares.

Place in a tightly sealed container to maintain softness. Enjoy!

Apple Spice Bars

Oh so moist and flavourful!

⅔ cup butter or margarine

1½ cups sugar

4 eggs

1½ cups flour

½ tsp salt

1 tsp baking powder

½ tsp baking soda

½ tsp nutmeg

½ tsp cinnamon

½ tsp ginger

2 cups apples, peeled and chopped

½ cup raisins, optional

Preheat oven to 350° F.

Cream butter and sugar in a large mixing bowl. Beat in eggs with an electric mixer.

In another bowl add flour, salt, baking powder, baking soda, nutmeg, cinnamon and ginger. Mix well.

Blend dry ingredients to the creamed mixture and mix well until blended.

Stir in chopped apples and raisins. Spread in a 13 by 9 inch greased cake pan.

Bake until golden or until toothpick inserted in center comes out clean. Let cool and cut into squares.

Can be stored in the refrigerator. Makes about 24 squares.

Date Squares

These squares are great for a special occasion!

2 cups flour

2 cups quick rolled oats

1½ cups brown sugar

1 cup butter or margarine

1 egg

1 tsp baking soda

3 cups dates, cut-up pitted (1 pound)

1½ cups water

Preheat oven to 350° F.

In a large bowl mix flour, oats, brown sugar, butter, egg and soda. Mix well until crumbly. Press half of the crumb mixture in a 13 by 9 inch greased cake pan evenly.

In a saucepan bring dates and water to a boil over low heat for about 10 minutes, constantly stirring, until thickened. Spread the date mixture on top of base evenly. Top with remaining crumb mixture.

Bake for about 30 minutes. Cool slightly and cut into squares and store in a sealed container.

Raisin Squares

Moist and chewy, what a treat!

2 cups flour

2 cups quick rolled oats

1½ cups brown sugar

1 cup butter or margarine

1 egg

1 tsp baking soda

2 cups raisins

1 can condensed milk

1 tbsp lemon juice

Preheat oven to 350°F.

In a large bowl mix flour, oats, brown sugar, butter, egg and baking soda. Mix well until crumbly. Press half of the crumb mixture in a 13 by 9 inch greased cake pan evenly.

In another bowl mix raisins, condensed milk, and lemon juice. Spread mixture evenly over crumb mixture. Top with remaining crumb mixture.

Bake for about 30 minutes. Cool slightly and cut into squares and store in a tightly sealed container.

Chocolate Chip Squares

One of the kid's favourites!

2 ¾ cups flour

2 tsp baking powder

3 eggs

1 cup sugar

¾ cup vegetable oil

1 tsp lemon juice

1 tsp vanilla

½ cup chocolate chips

½ cup walnuts, chopped

¼ tsp cinnamon

¼ cup sugar

Preheat oven to 350° F.

In a small bowl mix flour and baking powder, set aside. In a large mixing bowl beat eggs and sugar until yellow and thick using an electric mixer. Beat in vegetable oil, lemon juice, and vanilla. Beat for 1 minute. Then stir in dry ingredients. Add in chocolate chips and walnuts. Spread mixture evenly in a 13 by 9 inch greased cake pan.

In a small bowl mix ¼ cup sugar and cinnamon together. Sprinkle the sugar mixture over the squares. Bake for about 15-20 minutes or until golden in colour. Cool slightly, and cut into squares. Enjoy while warm.

Coffee Cake

The taste of mini sugared donuts!

⅔ cup butter or margarine

1 cup sugar

2 eggs

3 cups flour

4 tsp baking powder

½ tsp salt

1½ cups milk

TOPPING

1 cup brown sugar

3 tbsp flour

2 tbsp cinnamon

6 tbsp butter or margarine, melted

Preheat oven to 350°F.

In a large mixing bowl cream butter, sugar and eggs together.

In another bowl mix flour, baking powder and salt together.

Alternately add flour mixture then milk, doing this twice. Spread in a 13 by 9 inch greased cake pan evenly. Combine toppings in a bowl and sprinkle over batter. Bake for about 40 minutes or until an inserted toothpick comes out clean. Serve while warm.

Caramel Blueberry Coffee Cake

The taste of caramel and blueberries is just so scrumptious!

2 cups flour

½ cup sugar

3 tsp baking powder

½ tsp cinnamon

¼ tsp salt

2 eggs

¾ cup milk

¼ cup canola oil or vegetable oil

1¼ cups blueberries, fresh or frozen

TOPPING

¼ cup flour

¼ cup brown sugar

1 tsp cinnamon

2 tbsp butter, soft

2 tbsp caramel sauce topping

Preheat oven to 350°F.

In a large mixing bowl add flour, sugar, baking powder, cinnamon, and salt. Mix well and set aside.

In another mixing bowl beat eggs well using a whisk. Stir in milk and oil.

Pour this mixture into the dry ingredients.

Only mix to blend. Stir in blueberries.

Spread in a 13 by 9 inch greased cake pan evenly.

In a small bowl mix flour, brown sugar, cinnamon, and butter.

Sprinkle evenly on the top of the cake. Bake in oven for 20 minutes or until top of cake is golden in colour. Cool cake for five minutes and then pour caramel topping over the cake. Serve with ice cream when warm.

Basic White Cake

This cake is delicious on it's own!

2 cups flour

1½ cups sugar

3 tsp baking powder

½ tsp salt

1 cup milk

½ cup shortening

1 tsp vanilla

5 egg whites

Preheat oven to 350°F.

In a large bowl mix flour, sugar, baking powder, salt, milk and shortening.

Beat on medium speed using a hand mixer for 2 minutes.

Add vanilla and egg whites; continue beating for an additional 2 minutes.

Pour into a greased 13 by 9 inch cake pan or into two greased 9-inch round cake pans.

Bake for 30 minutes or until toothpick inserted comes out clean. Cool completely. Fill or frost as desired.

Best Ever Chocolate Cake

A chocoholic's delight!

2 ¼ cups flour

1⅔ cups sugar

¾ cup shortening

⅔ cup cocoa

1½ cups water

1¼ tsp baking soda

½ tsp salt

1 tsp vanilla

¼ tsp baking powder

2 eggs

Preheat oven to 350°F.

In a large mixing bowl beat all ingredients with electric mixer, on low speed for 30 seconds.

Beat for an additional 3 minutes on high speed, making sure you scrape the sides of the bowl. Pour into a greased 13 by 9 inch cake pan or into two greased 9-inch round cake pans. Bake for 30-40 minutes or until toothpick inserted comes out clean. Cool completely. Fill or frost as desired.

Marble Pound Cake

1¼ cups flour

1 cup cornstarch

3 tsp baking powder

¼ cup sugar

3 tbsp cocoa

¾ cup butter

1 cup sugar

4 egg yolks

1 cup milk

4 egg whites

In a medium bowl stir flour, cornstarch, and baking powder, set aside.

In another bowl thoroughly blend cocoa and ¼ cup sugar, set aside.

In a large bowl cream together ¾ cup butter and 1 cup sugar; beat in egg yolks.

Mix in flour mixture, alternating with the milk, ending with the dry ingredients.

Divide batter in half. Add to one of the halves the cocoa mixture.

In another bowl, beat egg whites until soft peaks form, about 5 minutes; divide egg whites in half and fold egg whites into each portion of batter.

Drop batter alternately by tablespoonfuls into a greased bundt pan. Use a knife and run it through the batter to make a marbleized effect. Bake in a 350°F oven for 50 to 60 minutes or until a toothpick inserted in center comes out clean.

Custard Cake

You will be amazed at how this cake forms two distinct layers. The cake layer will appear on the bottom and the custard will form on top.

CARAMEL

½ cup sugar

CUSTARD

4 cups water

6 eggs

½ cup sugar

1 tsp vanilla

2 cups powdered milk

CAKE

1 package white cake mix

In a small saucepan add the ½ cup sugar and cook over medium heat. Stir until sugar has melted and becomes a light golden brown. Be careful not to burn the sugar. Spread the browned sugar in a large cake pan. Set aside.

Prepare cake mix according to package directions. Set aside.

In a large bowl mix all the custard ingredients. Set aside.

Heat oven to 350°F; pour custard mixture on top of caramelized sugar; pour cake mixture on top of custard mixture. The cake needs to be cooked in a water bath; therefore place the custard cake pan in a larger pan and pour hot water in the empty pan.

Bake until knife inserted in center comes out clean. Cool and refrigerate until set. When ready to serve, flip cake upside down on a serving platter.

Carrot Cake

Such a moist cake!

1½ cups sugar

1 cup vegetable oil

3 eggs

2 cups flour

1 tsp cinnamon

1 tsp baking soda

1 tsp vanilla

½ tsp salt

¼ tsp nutmeg

3 cups carrots, peeled and shredded

1 cup walnuts, chopped (optional)

Preheat oven to 350°F.

In a large mixing bowl add sugar, oil and eggs, beating well. Stir in flour, cinnamon, baking soda, vanilla, salt and nutmeg. Add in shredded carrots and walnuts, stirring well.

Pour into a greased 13 by 9 inch cake pan. Bake for 40 to 45 minutes or until toothpick inserted comes out clean. Cool completely and ice with cream cheese icing or white icing.

Cream Cheese Icing

1 package cream cheese, softened (250g)

1 tsp vanilla

1 tbsp milk

4 cups icing sugar

In a mixing bowl beat cream cheese, vanilla, milk and 2 cups of icing sugar with an electric mixer. Add in the remainder of the icing sugar and beat until smooth.

White Icing

3 cups icing sugar

¼ cup butter or margarine, softened

2 tsp vanilla

2 to 3 tbsp milk

Mix all ingredients except milk in a mixing bowl. Beat until smooth.

When adding milk add a tablespoon at a time to see how much milk is required.

Beat until smooth. Can be used on any type of cake or cupcakes

Chocolate Carrot Cake

What a combination!

2 cups flour

1½ cups sugar

1 cup vegetable oil

½ cup orange juice

¼ cup cocoa

2 tsp baking soda

1 tsp salt

1 tsp cinnamon

1 tsp vanilla

4 eggs

2 ½ cups carrots, peeled and shredded

¼ cup coconut

¼ cup raisins

¼ cup walnuts, chopped

Preheat oven to 350°F.

In a large mixing bowl beat first ten ingredients just until blended with an electric mixer. Beat on high for 2 minutes. Add in carrots, coconut, raisins and walnuts, stirring well.

Pour into a greased 12-cup bundt cake pan or into a greased 13 by 9 inch cake pan. Bake for 50-55 minutes or until toothpick inserted comes out clean. Cool cake, if preferred can be iced with your choice of icing.

Banana Cake

2 ½ cups flour

1 tsp baking powder

1½ tsp baking soda

½ cup margarine, softened

1⅓ cups sugar

½ cup milk

1 tbsp lemon juice

2 eggs

1½ cups bananas, (mashed) about 3 mediums

½ cup walnuts, chopped

Preheat oven to 350°F.

In a large bowl mix all ingredients except nuts. Beat well using an electric mixer for 2 minutes on high.

Add in walnuts. Pour into a greased 13 by 9 inch cake pan.

Bake for 45 minutes or until toothpick inserted comes out clean. Cool cake and ice if preferred.

Banana Chocolate Chip Loaf

Best-banana loaf ever!

½ cup butter or margarine

1 cup sugar

2 eggs

1 cup bananas (ripe and mashed, about 3)

2 cups flour

1 tsp baking soda

½ tsp baking powder

¼ tsp salt

¼ tsp cinnamon

½ cup walnuts

½ cup chocolate chips

Preheat oven to 350°F.

In a large mixing bowl cream butter and sugar together. Beat in eggs until smooth using an electric mixer. Add mashed bananas and stir well.

In another bowl mix flour, baking soda, baking powder, salt and cinnamon.

Add to banana mixture. Stir until moist. Add walnuts and chocolate chips if desired.

Pour batter into a greased 9 by 5 by 3 inch loaf pan.

Bake for about 1 hour or until toothpick inserted comes out clean. Cool and cut into slices.

Apple Loaf

This loaf is great when apples are plentiful!

½ cup butter or margarine

1 cup sugar

2 eggs

1 tsp vanilla

1 cup apples (peeled and shredded)

2 cups flour

1 tsp baking powder

½ tsp baking soda

¼ tsp salt

½ tsp cinnamon

Preheat oven to 350°F.

In a large mixing bowl cream butter and sugar. Beat in eggs and vanilla using an electric mixer. Add in shredded apples, mixing well.

In another bowl mix flour, baking powder, baking soda, salt and cinnamon. Add into batter and mix only until moist. Pour into a greased 9 by 5 by 3 inch loaf pan.

Bake for about 1 hour or until toothpick inserted comes out clean. Cool and cut into slices.

Banana Chocolate Chip Muffins

The chocolate melts in your mouth when eaten warm!

1¾ cups flour

½ cup sugar

3 tsp baking powder

¼ tsp salt

½ tsp cinnamon

1 egg

¼ cup canola oil

¼ cup milk

1 cup bananas, mashed (3 medium)

¾ cup chocolate chips

½ cup walnuts, chopped (optional)

Preheat oven to 400°F.

In large mixing bowl, mix flour, sugar, baking powder, salt and cinnamon. Set aside.

In another bowl beat egg, oil, milk, and mashed bananas.

Pour dry mixture into egg mixture. Stir only until blended. Add chocolate chips and nuts if desired.

Fill greased muffin tins ¾ full. Bake for 20-25 minutes or until golden on top.

Best Blueberry Muffins

What a treat when eaten warm!

1¾ cups flour

3 tsp baking powder

¼ tsp salt

½ tsp cinnamon

¼ cup butter, softened

½ cup sugar

1 egg

¾ cup milk

1 tsp vanilla

1 cup blueberries, fresh or frozen

¼ cup brown sugar

Preheat oven to 400°F.

In a small mixing bowl, add flour, baking powder, salt and cinnamon, mix well. Set aside.

In another bowl, cream butter and sugar. Beat in egg, milk, and vanilla. Add in dry ingredients. Mixing just until blended.

Add in blueberries and mix well.

Fill greased muffin cups ¾ full. Sprinkle brown sugar on the tops of the muffins. Bake for 20 minutes or until golden brown on the top.

Pineapple Shortbread Treats

A tropical delight!

1 cup margarine, softened

⅓ cup cream cheese, softened

1 cup sugar

1 egg

2 tbsp frozen orange juice

2 ½ cups flour

1 tsp baking powder

1 can pineapple, crushed (drained, 8 ½ oz)

Preheat oven to 375°F.

In a large mixing bowl cream margarine, cream cheese and sugar. Beat in egg and frozen juice. In another bowl mix flour and baking powder together then add to creamed mixture.

Mix in drained pineapple, mixing well. Chill dough for 30 minutes.

Drop by tablespoonfuls 2 inches apart onto cookie sheets. Bake for 10 to 12 minutes or until lightly golden in color.

Chocolate Waffle Drops

A light and fluffy treat!

½ cup butter or margarine, softened
⅔ cup sugar
2 eggs
1 tsp vanilla
1¼ cups flour
¼ cup cocoa
1 tsp baking powder
¼ tsp salt
½ tsp cinnamon
½ cup walnuts, chopped

Preheat oven to 350°F.

In a large mixing bowl cream butter and sugar. Beat in eggs and vanilla, using an electric mixer.

In another bowl mix flour, cocoa, baking powder, salt and cinnamon. Add flour mixture to the creamed mixture, mixing well. Stir in walnuts.

Drop by teaspoonfuls 2 inches apart onto cookie sheet. Bake for 10 to 12 minutes or until set. Let cool and store in a tightly sealed container.

Buttery Tarts

Scrumptious and chewy!

3 eggs

1 cup corn syrup

1 cup sugar

2 tbsp butter, melted

1 tsp vanilla

1¼ cups raisins

24 tart shells, thawed (3 inch)

Preheat oven to 350°F.

In a mixing bowl beat eggs just until blended, over beating will spoil texture. Add in corn syrup, sugar, melted butter and vanilla. Mix gently until blended.

Take a large cookie tray and arrange tart shells. Spoon a tablespoon of raisins in each tart. Pour egg mixture into each tart, filling each tart ⅔ full. Bake in oven for 20 to 25 minutes or until golden and set. Cool and place in a tightly sealed container.

For Pecan Tarts: Omit raisins. Add 2 cups chopped pecans in tart shells.

Cream Cheese Tarts

3 pkgs cream cheese (250g)

1 cup sugar

3 tbsp flour

4 eggs

1½ tsp vanilla

1 cup whipping cream

24 tart shells, thawed (3 inch)

Preheat oven to 350°F.

In a large mixing bowl blend first six ingredients until smooth, using an electric hand mixer. Arrange tart shells on a large cookie tray. Place filling into each tart ⅔ full. Bake in oven for 15-20 minutes, until golden brown and until toothpick inserted comes out clean.

Truffles

Great on a party tray!

1 cup chocolate chips
½ cup sour cream
3 cups Graham cracker crumbs
½ cup icing sugar
2 tbsp corn syrup
1 cup pecans, chopped
coatings: ground pecans, ground walnuts or icing sugar

In a medium saucepan heat chocolate chips and sour cream on low heat, stirring constantly until smooth.

Place chocolate chip mixture in a large bowl. Add in Graham cracker crumbs, icing sugar, corn syrup and chopped pecans. Mix well.

Roll into 1½-inch balls. Roll each ball into desired coating.

Chill in refrigerator in a plastic covered container. Makes about 52 balls.

Mini Cheesecakes

Oh, so delicious!

1⅓ cups Graham cracker crumbs

⅓ cup butter or margarine, melted

¼ cup sugar

2 pkgs cream cheese, light (250g)

¾ cup sugar

2 eggs

1 tsp vanilla

½ cup chocolate chips, optional

Preheat oven to 325°F.

Line ungreased muffin cup pan with large paper liners.

In a large mixing bowl add graham cracker crumbs, melted butter and ¼ cup sugar. Mix well. Press evenly in bottom of each muffin cup.

In a medium bowl beat cream cheese and ¾ cup sugar until smooth, using an electric mixer. Beat in eggs and vanilla, blending well. Spoon filling evenly over prepared crusts.

Bake for 25 to 30 minutes, until set. Cool and then chill.

Chocolate cheesecakes: melt chocolate chips in a saucepan, stirring constantly. Add this to the batter and bake as directed.

Marble cheesecakes: melt two tablespoons chocolate chips on low heat in a saucepan. Take 3 tablespoons of batter and mix it with the melted chocolate. Pour the white batter evenly over the crusts then drop ½ teaspoon of chocolate batter into each one. Take a toothpick and make a zigzag pattern. Bake as directed.

Cherry Cheesecake

Fatat's Special! Dedicated to my daughter, Souad Hammoud, who has inspired and motivated me in so many ways.

2 cups Graham crumbs

½ cup butter or margarine, melted

1 pkg cream cheese, room temperature

½ cup brown sugar

3 eggs, room temperature

2 tsp vanilla

½ litre whipped cream dessert topping, thawed

1 can cherry topping filling

Preheat oven to 450°F.

In a mixing bowl mix crumbs and butter until mixed well. Press firmly in bottom of 9-inch spring form pan.

In a large mixing bowl beat cream cheese until smooth using an electric mixer.

Beat in brown sugar. Beat 1 egg at a time on low speed mixing just until blended.

Add vanilla and whipped cream, beat until smooth. Pour into crust-lined pan.

Bake for 10 minutes at 450°F then lower oven to 250°F; bake for an additional 60 minutes or until set.

Let cool for 10 minutes and remove sides of pan. Cool completely.

Top with cherry topping or the topping of choice.

Refrigerate for at least 4 hours before serving. Keep refrigerated.

Tip

Just before placing cheesecake in the oven, on the bottom rack place a 13 by 9 inch glass baking pan filled half full of water. This allows the cheesecake to bake without cracking at the top.

Cherry Cups

What a decadent dessert!

8 frozen phyllo pastry sheets, thawed

1 cup butter, melted

1 pkg cream cheese, softened (250g)

2 tbsp sugar

1 tbsp lemon juice

½ tsp lemon rind, grated

1 cup whipped cream, thawed

1 can cherry topping

Preheat oven to 350°F.

Lay phyllo sheets on cleaned counter. Cover with clean tea towel, to prevent drying.

Take 4 phyllo sheets at a time and brush 1 sheet of phyllo pastry with melted butter; top with another phyllo dough sheet and repeat until all 4 sheets are done.

Cut into 12 square pieces. Place into a 12-cup muffin pan. With fingers press pastry down in each cup and press into a cup shape and ensuring sides are pinched. Repeat these steps for the remaining phyllo pastry sheets. Bake for 10-15 minutes, until golden brown. Let cool.

In a large mixing bowl mix cream cheese, sugar, lemon juice, and rind and whipped cream until smooth. Fill cooled pastries with one tablespoon of filling. Top with cherry topping. Refrigerate until use. Makes 24.

Baklava

*Dedicated to our father, Hussien Ayache, whose words of wisdom and guidance
will always resonate in our hearts.*

1 cup walnuts, chopped

½ cup almonds, chopped

½ cup pistachios, chopped

½ cup cashews, chopped

½ cup sugar

2 tbsp cinnamon

2 tbsp rose water

2 cups butter, unsalted and melted

1 pkg frozen phyllo pastry sheets, thawed

2 syrup recipes (see recipe below)

Preheat oven to 300°F.

In a large mixing bowl mix walnuts, almonds, pistachios, cashews, sugar, cinnamon and rose water, mixing well. Set aside filling.

Butter the bottom of a 14 by 10 inch baking pan. Split phyllo sheets in half, one part for the top and the other for the bottom. Cover sheets so they would not get dry with a clean tea towel.

Start by placing one phyllo sheet on bottom of the pan. Brush butter on the sheet and keep repeating until half of sheets are buttered. Spread filling evenly over buttered sheets. Place a phyllo sheet over filling and brush with butter. Repeat until all sheets are buttered, making sure top sheet is buttered well.

Cut baklava into shape desired, either diamond or square shaped and bake for approximately an hour or until golden brown. Once removed from oven, pour cold syrup over the baklava and top with ground pistachios. If more syrup is needed, more can be added by making another recipe.

Syrup

This recipe is used for a lot of sweets

4 cups sugar

2 cups water

½ lemon, squeezed

1 tbsp rose water

In a large pot bring sugar and water to a boil on medium heat. Once it starts to boil, add in lemon juice. Let boil for 5 minutes, and then add in rose water. Let boil for an extra 5 minutes. Let cool. Syrup should be slightly thick.

Shaybiyat –
Baklava Filled With Cream

1 pkg phyllo pastry dough
2 cups unsalted butter, melted
2 syrup recipes, (page 197)

FILLING:
2 cups whipping cream
⅓ cup sugar
⅓ cup cornstarch
½ cup milk

If phyllo dough is frozen thaw out for 4-5 hours.

Filling: Pour whipping cream into small pot. Mix cornstarch and milk in a bowl. Then add to whipping cream and stir on LOW HEAT. Add sugar to mixture and stir constantly until becomes thick. Remove from heat.

Roll out the phyllo dough keeping the parchment paper underneath it on a damp cloth. Determine the size you would like the Shaybiyat to be 4cm, 5cm or larger. Measure out dough to the desired size and begin cutting gently with a butter knife, measuring either horizontally or vertically as long as the measurements are the same, ending up with a square shape. Brush butter on the bottom of each square and at the top of each square. It is better to do one square at a time.

Put filling in the center of the square. For a smaller square put ½ tsp to 1 tsp of filling and for a larger square put 1 tbsp, making sure not to add too much filling as it will overflow while baking. Fold over into a triangle pressing sides together. Take each side and dip it into the butter making sure to cover it all in butter and then press all sides again. Place on a baking sheet. Once all the triangles are all finished, brush tops with butter once more before putting in oven. Preheat oven to 350°F. Bake on middle rack until lightly browned on top and bottom. Approximately 15-20 minutes. Remove and cool for 5 minutes. Pour syrup over each triangle coating it well. Once all triangles are coated with syrup, let sit for 5 minutes and then remove to a tray. It is best not to cover Shaybiyat at all. If more syrup is desired, more can be added later individually.

Ma'amoul

8 cups semolina or cream of wheat

2 cups unsalted butter, melted and cooled

¼ cup sugar

½ tsp instant yeast

milk, lukewarm (about 2 cups)

icing sugar

FILLING:

2 cups walnuts, finely chopped

1 cup pistachios, finely chopped

1 tsp ground cinnamon

1 tsp ground nutmeg

¼ to ½ cup brown sugar

2 tbsp orange blossom water

In a large bowl, add the semolina and melted butter. Rub and mix well with hands. Cover and set aside for 6 hours.

Combine the filling ingredients and set aside.

In a saucepan, warm the milk then add the sugar and yeast. Set aside for 5 minutes. Mix the semolina mixture with your hands, and then slowly add the milk mixture as you mix and knead the mixture with your hands. You may need more or less milk, use your judgement. The mixture will resemble pie dough and it will be soft and pliable. Cover and set aside.

Preheat oven to 300°F.

To make filling, add all the filling ingredients in a bowl and mix well.

To form Ma'amoul, take a small amount of mixture, the size of a walnut, and shape into a ball. Make a cavity in the center and place 1 teaspoon of nut filling inside. Close the cavity, sealing well. Place the walnut filled ball into a decorative mold, (usually known as a Tabih) pressing the ball gently. Turn the mold upside down; with one hand underneath. Give the top edge of the mold a gentle tap on the counter top, the ma'amoul should fall out. Place on a baking tray, flat side down and the domed shape up.

Bake for 25 to 30 minutes. The ma'amoul should be a light brown. Allow to cool well. Sprinkle icing sugar on top of each ma'amoul; Store in an airtight container.

Ma'amoul with Dates

Lebanese version of Date Filled Cookies!

DOUGH:

4 cups flour

1 cup semolina or cream of wheat

2 tsp baking powder

1 tsp vanilla

1 cup butter

½ cup vegetable oil

¼ cup sugar

1 tbsp orange blossom water

¾ cup warm milk

FILLING:

2 cups pressed pitted dates

½ tsp cinnamon (optional)

2 tbsp orange blossom water

½ cup butter, softened

Preheat oven to 350°F.

Prepare the filling by combining all the filling ingredients in a saucepan. Heat through, remove and place in a food processor. Blend until smooth, remove and set aside.

To prepare the dough, use a mixer with a kneading hook and knead ingredients for 3 minutes until it forms a smooth dough.

To form cookies, pinch off small pieces of dough and make a cavity in the center of each piece.

Place a teaspoon of the date filling inside of the cavity, seal and place dough ball inside of "Tabih" a special mold for making Ma'amoul (if you do not have one, place ball on baking sheet and use a fork to decorate) press dough in mold, turn mold upside down and gently tap the edge of the mold onto your work surface. Be prepared to catch the cookie as it falls out of the mold.

Place the cookies onto a baking sheet, keeping spaces between each cookie. Bake for 20 minutes or until light golden brown. Store in an airtight container, once cooled.

Cream of Wheat Squares

Hareesee, also known as Namura, are easy to make and are exceptionally good on a special occasion!

Kefah's Special: dedicated to my mom, Adele Abdallah, who inspired and taught me to put my heart into cooking.

3 cups cream of wheat or semolina

½ cup sugar

3 tsp baking powder

3 tsp rose water

½ cup coconut

1 tsp orange extract

1 cup yogurt, plain

24 almonds, whole, blanched

1 syrup recipe, (page 197)

Preheat oven to 350°F.

In a large mixing bowl add cream of wheat, sugar, baking powder, rose water, coconut and orange extract. Mix well, blending ingredients together.

Mix in yogurt, if more is needed add a bit more. It should be soft and pliable.

Pour into a 13 by 9 inch greased cake pan. Lightly press knife to mark 24 squares, making sure not to cut through.

Place almonds in the middle of each square. Bake until top is golden brown.

Immediately cut through squares where marked and pour syrup over the squares evenly.

Cover cake pan with tin foil, this allows the squares to soften and for the syrup to be absorbed.

Cool and store in a tightly sealed container. Makes 24 squares.

Anise Seed Squares

Yanasoon squares!

1 cup vegetable oil

1 cup sugar

3 eggs

1 tsp vanilla

2 cups flour

1 tsp baking powder

2 tsp anise seeds, yanasoon

Preheat oven to 350°F.

In a large mixing bowl mix oil and sugar together. Add in eggs and vanilla, beating with a large wooden spoon. Add in flour, baking powder and anise seeds. Mix well until blended.

Pour into a greased 13 by 9 inch cake pan. Bake until golden brown.

Cool and then cut into squares or long fingers. Store in a tightly sealed container to stay soft.

Macaroni Pastries

These are exceptionally good on Eid!

½ tsp yeast

1 cup water

6 cups flour

1 cup cornstarch

½ tsp cinnamon

½ tsp nutmeg

½ tsp anise seed, (yanasoon)

½ tsp baking powder

1½ cups vegetable oil

vegetable oil for frying

1 recipe of cold syrup (page 197)

Mix water and yeast together, set aside. Mix flour, cornstarch, spices and baking powder in a bowl. Add oil and mix together well, add more if needed.

Add yeast and water, mix well. Knead dough until it is tough and add a bit more oil if necessary.

Cover for half an hour until dough rises.

Take about a tablespoon of the dough and to shape use a large strainer with large holes (colander) and take dough and roll dough into a long finger shape on strainer to get the design. Repeat with the rest of the dough.

In a frying pan, heat oil and fry pastries until golden brown. Drop into cold syrup immediately for about one minute, then remove and let cool before serving. Repeat this step for the rest of the pastries.

Ghrabi – Lebanese Shortbread

So lovely on a party tray!

2 cups unsalted butter, softened
1¼ cups icing sugar
1 tbsp cornstarch
1 tbsp vanilla or vanilla sugar
flour, as much as needed

In a mixing bowl add butter, icing sugar, cornstarch, and vanilla. Mix well. Add in flour, a little at a time just until mixture is pliable like pie dough.

On a cookie sheet shape cookies into a circle and flatten or use a special tabbeh, a designed mold for ghrabi, and bake in oven at 350°F until bottoms are slightly brown, making sure not to over bake.

Cool and remove from cookie sheet and store in a sealed container until ready to serve.

Shredded Pastry Squares – Knafee

These squares are filled with a delicious cream!

1 cup butter, unsalted, melted
1 pkg frozen shredded pastry dough, thawed
2 cups whip cream, liquid (½ litre)
⅓ cup cornstarch
½ cup milk
¼ cup sugar
1 syrup (recipe below)

Preheat oven to 350°F.

Grease a 13 by 9 inch cake pan. In a large mixing bowl piece shredded pastry dough into small pieces by hand. Pour melted butter over the dough making sure all dough is covered. Split the dough into two. Spread one half into greased pan and set the other half aside.

In a saucepan pour whip cream. In a small bowl add cornstarch and milk and mix well together until there are no lumps and smooth. Add to whip cream and then add sugar. Stir on low heat and constantly stirring until thickened and bubbly. Pour evenly onto dough in pan. Top with other half of dough, spreading evenly. Bake until golden brown, about 30 minutes.

Once baked, pour syrup over the squares evenly. Cover with a piece of tin foil to allow syrup to be absorbed and squares to soften. Cut when cooled.

Syrup

3 cups sugar
1½ cups water
½ lemon, squeezed
2 tbsp rose water

In a large pot add sugar and water; let it come to a boil over medium heat. Add in lemon and let boil for 5 minutes. Add in rose water and boil for extra 5 minutes. Syrup should be slightly thick.

Lebanese Cookies – Kaak

Use your imagination to make the shape you want, recipe can be doubled!

½ cup butter or margarine (unsalted, melted)

1 cup sugar

½ cup vegetable oil

1 cup yogurt, plain

3 eggs, beaten

1 tsp vanilla

1 tbsp rose water

1 tbsp baking powder

¼ tsp baking soda

½ tsp cinnamon

½ tsp nutmeg

flour, as needed

Preheat oven to 350°F.

In a large mixing bowl add melted butter, sugar, oil, yogurt, eggs, vanilla and rose water. Blend well.

Add in baking powder, baking soda, cinnamon, nutmeg and a cup of flour at a time. Mix with hands kneading well and adding more flour until dough is the consistency of pie dough.

Take pieces of dough the size of preference and roll into a long rope and wrap into a circle. Using a special designed mold (tabih) flatten slightly dough to make pattern, or just keep round, slightly flatten with fingers and place on cookie sheet.

Place cookies two inches apart and bake until golden. Cool slightly and store in a tightly sealed container.

Date Filled Cookies – Arass Bi Ajwee

Dedicated to our mother, Suhila Ayache, whose generosity and kindness outshines us all.

2 cups butter (unsalted, melted)

2 cups sugar

¼ cup milk, warmed

3 eggs, beaten

1 tsp vanilla

1 tbsp mahleb

1 tbsp rose water

1½ tsp baking powder

5 cups flour

3 cups dates, chopped

1½ cups water

Preheat oven to 350°F.

In a large mixing bowl mix butter, sugar, and milk together. Add in eggs, vanilla, mahleb, and rose water, blending well. Mix in baking powder and flour. If more flour is needed then add more. Dough should be soft and pliable.

In a saucepan put dates and water and let boil over low heat until dates become soft.

Take a piece of dough and make it into a round ball. Make a cavity in the middle with your finger and put a half-teaspoon of date filling in the dough. Close cavity, trying not to get filling on the outside of dough. Put in special mold (tabih) and place two inches apart on cookie sheet.

Bake until cookies are golden. Cool and store in a tightly sealed container.

Atayif

ATAYIF BATTER:

2 cups flour

1 tsp baking soda

½ tsp baking powder

1 tsp sugar

½ tsp salt

1 large egg, beaten

water, as much as needed

FILLING:

1 cup ricotta cheese

½ cup mozzarella cheese, shredded

¼ cup sugar

1 tbsp orange blossom water

butter or cooking spray

1 cup shelled pistachios, chopped fine in a food processor

SYRUP

4 cups sugar

2 cups water

1 tsp lemon juice

½ tsp rose water or orange blossom water

Start by preparing the syrup; in a saucepan add the sugar and water. Stir until sugar dissolves. Bring to a boil; add lemon juice and boil for 10 minutes on medium heat. Add the rose water or orange blossom water and boil for an additional 5 minutes. Cool and refrigerate until ready to use.

To make the **Atayif batter**, start by mixing together the dry ingredients. Stir in the egg; add water and mix until you have a thin pancake batter; it will resemble a crepe batter.

Heat a griddle or large frying pan on medium heat and grease lightly. Spread 1 tbsp of batter and use the back of a spoon to quickly form it into a 3" circle. Cook until bubbles appear and surface is almost dry. Do not flip and do not overcook. Remove Atayif from griddle and place in a single layer on a baking sheet or work surface. Continue with the remaining batter making as many as can be handled on the cooking surface.

For the filling; in a bowl, combine the ricotta, mozzarella cheese, sugar and blossom water. Fill each Atayif round with 1 teaspoon of ricotta mixture. Do not overfill. Fold in half and seal with your fingertips. You can freeze them in a single layer at this point until you are ready to use them.

Preheat oven to 400°F. Grease a baking pan and place Atayif in a single layer. Dab each Atayif with melted butter or spray with butter cooking spray. Bake for 20 to 30 minutes or until filling is hot. Remove from oven and immediately dip Atayif in cold syrup, remove Atayif from syrup onto a serving platter. Sprinkle with pistachios. Serve and enjoy!

Lebanese Atayif

ATAYIF BATTER:
1¼ cups water
½ tsp yeast
1 tsp sugar
2 cups flour
pinch of salt

SYRUP:
4 cups sugar
2 cups water
1 tsp lemon juice
½ tsp rose water or
orange blossom water

CHEESE FILLING:
1 cup ricotta cheese
1 tsp orange blossom water
½ tsp cinnamon
2 tbsp sugar
OR
NUT FILLING:
1 cup walnuts, chopped
¼ cup sugar
1 tsp cinnamon
1 tsp orange blossom

Start by preparing the syrup; in a saucepan add the sugar and water. Stir until sugar dissolves. Bring to a boil; add lemon juice and boil for 10 minutes on medium heat. Add the rose water or orange blossom water and boil for an additional 2 minutes. Cool and refrigerate until ready to use.

For the **Atayif batter**, Sprinkle the yeast and sugar over the water and set aside, until the yeast foams. Mix the flour and salt and add the yeast mixture. Stir to a smooth batter; Cover with plastic film; Set aside for two hours.

Heat a griddle or large frying pan on medium heat and grease lightly; spread 1-2 tbsp of batter and use the back of a spoon to quickly form it into a 3" circle. Cook until bubbles appear and surface is almost dry. Do not flip and do not overcook. Remove Atayif from griddle and place in a single layer on a baking sheet or work surface. Continue with the remaining batter making as many as can be handled on the cooking surface.

Mix the ingredients for the kind of filling wanted. Place a tablespoonful of the cheese or nut filling in the center of the uncooked side of each Atayif. Fold over and pinch the edges to form a half moon.

There are two ways of cooking the Atayif, either you can bake them or fry them. If you prefer frying, heat the oil for deep-frying and fry the filled Atayif in small batches for 2-3 minutes, until golden brown. Remove with a slotted spoon onto a plate lined with paper towels to absorb excess oil.

Pour the cold syrup into a deep bowl. Dip the hot Atayif in the cold syrup, remove and serve with a sprinkle of chopped or ground pistachios.

For **baked Atayif**, arrange the filled Atayif on a baking sheet, sprinkle with melted butter and bake for 10 to 15 minutes in a 400°F oven.

Pour the cold syrup into a deep bowl. Dip the hot Atayif in the cold syrup, remove and serve with a sprinkle of chopped or ground pistachios.

Barazik – Sesame cookies

4 cups flour

2 cups icing sugar

½ tsp mahleb

½ cup butter, melted

½ cup vegetable shortening, melted

¼ tsp yeast

2 egg yolks

warm milk (as needed)

TOPPING:

2 egg whites

1 tbsp sugar

½ lb sesame seeds

In a large bowl, mix the flour, icing sugar, and mahleb. Add the yeast, butter, shortening, and egg yolks; mix well. Warm milk and add a little at a time to the mixture until the mixture forms a soft dough.

In a small bowl mix the egg whites and sugar, set aside. Place the sesame seeds in a shallow bowl, set aside.

To form the cookies, take a small amount of the dough, about the size of a walnut, and form into a ball. Dip the dough ball into the egg mixture then into the sesame seeds, pressing to flatten. Place onto a cookie sheet, sesame side up. Repeat with remaining dough.

Bake until golden in a 350°F oven. Remove from baking sheet and allow to cool. Store in an airtight container.

Tahini (Sesame Seed Paste) Cookies

1¼ cups butter, softened

1 cup sugar

2 tsp vanilla

1 tsp cinnamon

1 tsp grated orange zest

¼ tsp salt

¾ cup tahini, sesame paste

3 cups flour

2 tsp baking powder

FOR DUSTING:

4 tbsp icing sugar

1½ tsp cinnamon

In a large bowl, beat with a hand mixer the butter and the sugar for 5 minutes until light and fluffy.

Add the vanilla, cinnamon, salt, orange zest and tahini. Beat to a smooth consistency.

Add the flour and baking powder and mix. Dough will be smooth and soft. Cover the dough and refrigerate for 1 hour.

Preheat oven to 350°F.

Mix the icing sugar and cinnamon, for dusting, in a small bowl and set aside.

Pinch small pieces (the size of large olives) from the dough and roll into a ball. Roll the balls into the icing sugar mixture and place on a parchment lined baking sheet, keeping spaces between each ball.

Bake for 15 minutes. The cookies will be very light in color. Allow to cool completely before removing from pan; store in an airtight container.

Rice Pudding

So creamy and satisfying!

½ cup water
5 cups milk
¾ cup rice, calrose style
½ cup sugar
1 tbsp cornstarch
¼ cup water
1 tbsp rosewater (optional)

Pour water and milk into a large pot. Set heat to low.

Wash rice and then add to milk. Add sugar, adding more or less to taste.

In a small bowl mix cornstarch with ¼ cup water and dissolve. Add it to the milk mixture.

Add rosewater if desired. Mix on low heat occasionally, making sure that the rice pudding does not scorch. Stir often making sure the rice does not stick to the bottom of pot.

Cook for approximately half an hour to an hour or until rice has cooked and pudding has thickened.

When the rice has cooked, transfer into serving size glass bowls.

Let cool and set. Top with nuts, shredded coconut, or raisins if desired.

Can be eaten warm or cold.

A

Ainar 24
Anise Seed Squares. 202

Appetizers, Dips and Drinks

Ainar. 24
Arabic Coffee. 27
Baba Ghanouj – Eggplant Dip 12
Bruschetta with Feta. 18
Caramel Popcorn 22
Chai 28
Cheese Ball. 15
Cheese Twists 18
Cinnamon Sugar Toasted Pecans 22
Citrus Punch. 24
Fish Sauce 14
Fool m'Dammas – Fava Bean Dip. 11
Fruit Cocktail 25
Garlic Sauce 13
Grilled Pita Bread. 14
Hot Chocolate. 28
Humous – Chickpea Dip 11
Layered Dip for Tortillas 16
Lemonade. 23
Orange Delight. 25
Pastry Bites. 19
Quick and Easy Guacamole 20
Raspberry Iced Tea. 23
Saudi Champagne. 23
Saudi Coffee. 27
Spinach Dip 19
Strawberry Vanilla Smoothie 26
Stuffed Mushrooms 17
Taratur - Tahini (Sesame Seed) Sauce 13
The Ultimate Smoothie Milk Shake. 26
Tomato Salsa 20
Yogurt Dip – Laban 21
Apple Loaf 187
Apple Spice Bars. 174
Arabic Coffee 27
Atayif 208

B

Baba Ghanouj – Eggplant Dip 12
Baked and Breaded Chicken. 90
Baked Chicken and Vegetables. 72
Baked Kibbi 118
Baked Stuffed Chicken 71
Baking Powder Biscuits 150
Baklava 197
Banana Bread 154
Banana Cake 185
Banana Chocolate Chip Loaf 186
Banana Chocolate Chip Muffins. 188
Banana Drops 168

Barazik Sesame cookies 210
Barbequed Chicken. 70
Basic Bread Dough 130
Basic Scones 152
Basic White Cake 179
Bass Fish with Cilantro Sauce 127
BBQ Salmon on Cedar Planks 120
Beef Broth 31
Beef Noodle Stew 35
Beef Stir Fry 103
Best Blueberry Muffins. 189
Best Ever Chocolate Cake 180

Breads

Baking Powder Biscuits 150
Banana Bread 154
Basic Bread Dough 130
Basic Scones. 152
Cheesy Garlic Bread 158
Cinnamon Sticky Buns. 155
Corn Bread Muffins 149
Danish Pastries 157
Delicate Tender Biscuits. 151
Feta Cheese Pies. 131
French Toast 153
Iranian Bread or Tanoor Bread. 143
Irresistible Meat Pies 133
Lebanese Bread 147
Mahamarah - Tomato Pies 137
Middle Eastern Cheese Bread 148
Naan Bread. 140
Naan Bread (Another version) 141
Pancakes. 153
Pizza. 139
Potato Pies 136
Powdered sugar glaze. 157
Roti 142
Saudi Style Meat Pies. 134
Skillet Meat Pockets. 144
Tangy Spinach Pies 132
Traditional Rolls. 156
Urban 146
Vegetable Stuffed Pockets 145
Zaatar Pies 138
Brownies. 169
Bruschetta with Feta 18
Burgers 100
Burghul and Chickpeas 59
Burghul and Tomatoes 60
Burghul Balls with Yogurt – Dahareej and Laban 61
Burghul Pilaf. 53
Buttery Tarts 192

C

Cabbage Rolls 106
Caesar Salad 48
Caramel Blueberry Coffee Cake 178
Caramel Popcorn 22
Carrot Cake 183
Chai 28
Cheese Ball 15
Cheese Twists 18
Cheesy Garlic Bread 158
Cherry Cheesecake 195
Cherry Cups 196

Chicken

Baked and Breaded Chicken 90
Baked Chicken and Vegetables 72
Baked Stuffed Chicken 71
Barbequed Chicken 70
Chicken and Linguine 96
Chicken and Vegetable Layer – Maaloobi 77
Chicken Bake Casserole 83
Chicken Broccoli Fettuccine 95
Chicken Burgers 81
Chicken Fajitas 81
Chicken in a Mushroom Cream Sauce 92
Chicken Pansett - Stir-Fry 91
Chicken Pot Pie 84
Chicken Quesadillas 82
Chicken Rice and Peas 76
Chicken Soup Bake 75
Chicken Souvlaki 85
Chicken Stir Fry 80
Creamy Chicken and Rice 76
Fried-Oven Chicken 70
Grilled Chicken Breasts 89
Lebanese Seasoned Baked Chicken 88
Lebanese Style Chicken Rolls 94
Maaloobi (Rice and Chicken) – Family Style 78
Mloukiah 86
Mloukiah with Chicken 87
Potato Stuffed Chicken 74
Roasted Glazed Chicken 93
Seasoned Chicken Breasts 73
Chicken and Linguine 96
Chicken and Vegetable Layer – Maaloobi 77
Chicken Bake Casserole 83
Chicken Broccoli Fettuccine 95
Chicken Broth 32
Chicken Burgers 81
Chicken Fajitas 81
Chicken in a Mushroom Cream Sauce 92
Chicken Noodle Soup 33
Chicken Pansett - Stir-Fry 91
Chicken Pot Pie 84
Chicken Quesadillas 82

Chicken Rice and Peas 76
Chicken Soup Bake 75
Chicken Souvlaki 85
Chicken Stir Fry 80
Chili Stir Fry 105
Chocolate Carrot Cake 184
Chocolate Chip Cookies 161
Chocolate Chip Nut Cookies 162
Chocolate Chip Squares 176
Chocolate Icing 169
Chocolate Squares 172
Chocolate Waffle Drops 191
Cinnamon Sticky Buns 155
Cinnamon Sugar Toasted Pecans 22
Citrus Punch 24
Coffee Cake 177
Colourful Crab 126
Corn Bread Muffins 149
Cream Cheese Icing 183
Cream Cheese Tarts 192
Cream of Broccoli Soup 36
Cream of Wheat Squares 201
Creamy Chicken and Rice 76
Custard Cake 182

D

Danish Pastries 157
Date Filled Cookies – Arass Bi Ajwee 207
Date Squares 175
Deep Fried Shrimp 123
Delicate Tender Biscuits 151

Desserts

Anise Seed Squares 202
Apple Loaf 187
Apple Spice Bars 174
Atayif 208
Baklava 197
Banana Cake 185
Banana Chocolate Chip Loaf 186
Banana Chocolate Chip Muffins 188
Banana Drops 168
Barazik Sesame cookies 210
Basic White Cake 179
Best Blueberry Muffins 189
Best Ever Chocolate Cake 180
Brownies 169
Buttery Tarts 192
Caramel Blueberry Coffee Cake 178
Carrot Cake 183
Cherry Cheesecake 195
Cherry Cups 196
Chocolate Carrot Cake 184
Chocolate Chip Cookies 161
Chocolate Chip Nut Cookies 162

Chocolate Chip Squares 176
Chocolate Icing 169
Chocolate Squares 172
Chocolate Waffle Drops 191
Coffee Cake 177
Cream Cheese Icing 183
Cream Cheese Tarts 192
Cream of Wheat Squares 201
Custard Cake 182
Date Filled Cookies – Arass Bi Ajwee 207
Date Squares. 175
Double Chocolate Chip Cookies 164
Dream Bars. 171
Ghrabi-Lebanese Shortbread 204
Hermits. 165
Jam Squares 173
Lebanese Atayif 209
Lebanese Cookies Kaak 206
Ma'amoul. 199
Ma'amoul with Dates 200
Macaroni Pastries 203
Marble Pound Cake 181
Marshmallow Rice Squares 170
Mini Cheesecakes. 194
Oatmeal Chocolate Chip Cookies 163
Peanut Butter Cookies 166
Pecan Tarts 192
Pineapple Shortbread Treats. 190
Puffed Wheat Squares 170
Raisin Squares 175
Rice Pudding 212
Shaybiyat – Baklava Filled With Cream 198
Shortbread Cookies 167
Shredded Pastry Squares – Knafee 205
Sugar Cookies 167
Syrup 197
Tahini (Sesame Seed Paste) Cookies 211
Truffles. 193
White Icing. 183
Dilled Rice with Mixed Vegetables 55
Double Chocolate Chip Cookies. 164
Dream Bars 171

E

Egg Salad 46

F

Fattoush. 47
Feta Cheese Pies 131
Fetti – Pita bread and chick peas. 52

Fish

Bass Fish with Cilantro Sauce 127
BBQ Salmon on Cedar Planks 120
Colourful Crab 126
Deep- Fried Shrimp 123
Fried Fish, Egyptian Style 122
Halibut Bake. 128
Lobster in White Sauce 124
Salsa for Fish 120
Seafood Stew 125
Shrimp in Tomato Sauce 124
Simple Fried Fish 122
Stuffed Baked Fish. 121
Tuna Melts 126
Tuna Wraps 128
Fish Sauce 14
Fool m'Dammas – Fava Bean Dip 11
French Onion Soup 41
French Toast 153
Fried Fish, Egyptian Style. 122
Fried-Oven Chicken 70
Fruit Cocktail 25

G

Garden Salad 48
Garlic Sauce 13
Ghrabi-Lebanese Shortbread 204
Greek Salad. 43
Green Bean Stew. 108
Grilled Chicken Breasts 89
Grilled Pita Bread 14

H

Halibut Bake 128
Hermits 165
Hot Chocolate 28
Humous – Chickpea Dip. 11

I

Iranian Bread or Tanoor Bread 143
Irresistible Meat Pies. 133

J

Jam Squares 173

K

Kafta 101
Kafta with Potatoes 102
Kibbi Nayeh – Meat with crushed wheat 116
Kidney Bean Stew. 109
Kishk Soup 42

L

Lasagne 113
Layered Dip for Tortillas 16
Lebanese Atayif 209
Lebanese Bread 147
Lebanese Cookies Kaak 206
Lebanese Salad 49
Lebanese Seasoned Baked Chicken 88
Lebanese Style Chicken Rolls 94
Lemonade 23
Lentil (Addas) Soup 38
Lentils and Burghul 58
Lentils and Rice – Majadarra 57
Lentil Soup with Beef 39
Lentil Soup with Lemon 40
Lobster in White Sauce 124

M

Maaloobi (Rice and Chicken) – Family Style 78
Ma'amoul 199
Ma'amoul with Dates 200
Macaroni Pastries 203
Macaroni Salad 44
Mahamarah - Tomato Pies 137
Marble Pound Cake 181
Marshmallow Rice Squares 170
Mashed Potatoes 62
Meat Kabobs 99

Meatless Dishes

Burghul and Chickpeas 59
Burghul and Tomatoes 60
Burghul Balls with Yogurt – Dahareej and Laban 61
Burghul Pilaf 53
Dilled Rice with Mixed Vegetables 55
Fetti – Pita bread and chick peas 52
Lentils and Burghul 58
Lentils and Rice – Majadarra 57
Mashed Potatoes 62
Nut and Raisin Topping 54
Potato Casserole 62
Rice Pilaf 53
Rice with an Egyptian Flare 54
Spinach and Rice 63
Spinach Tortellini 67
Stuffed Grape Leaves – Warak Inaab 56
Tortellini Alfredo 65
Vegetable Tortellini 66
Zucchini and Eggs 64
Zucchini and Tomatoes 64
Meat Maaloobi 112

Meats

Baked Kibbi 118
Beef Stir Fry 103
Burgers 100
Cabbage Rolls 106
Chili Stir Fry 105
Green Bean Stew 108
Kafta 101
Kafta with Potatoes 102
Kibbi Nayeh – Meat with crushed wheat 116
Kidney Bean Stew 109
Lasagne 113
Meat Kabobs 99
Meat Maaloobi 112
Okra Stew – Bami 110
Roast Beef 98
Rotini in a Pan 115
Shepherd's Pie 111
Spaghetti 114
Stuffed Kibbi Balls 117
Stuffed Zucchini – Koussa Mihshee 107
Tacos 104
Middle Eastern Cheese Bread 148
Minestrone Soup 37
Mini Cheesecakes 194
Mloukiah 86
Mloukiah with Chicken 87

N

Naan Bread 140
Naan Bread (Another version) 141
No Mayo Coleslaw 44
Nut and Raisin Topping 54

O

Oatmeal Chocolate Chip Cookies 163
Okra Stew – Bami 110
Orange Delight 25

P

Pancakes 153
Pastry Bites 19
Peanut Butter Cookies 166
Pecan Tarts 192
Pineapple Shortbread Treats 190
Pizza 139
Potato and Egg Salad 46
Potato Casserole 62
Potato Pies 136
Potato Salad 45
Potato Stuffed Chicken 74
Powdered sugar glaze 157
Puffed Wheat Squares 170

Q

Quick and Easy Guacamole 20

R

Raisin Squares. 175
Raspberry Iced Tea 23
Rice Pilaf. 53
Rice Pudding. 212
Rice with an Egyptian Flare 54
Roast Beef. 98
Roasted Glazed Chicken 93
Roti 142
Rotini in a Pan. 115

S

Salsa for Fish. 120
Saudi Champagne 23
Saudi Coffee 27
Saudi Style Meat Pies 134
Seafood Stew 125
Seasoned Chicken Breasts 73
Shaybiyat – Baklava Filled With Cream. 198
Shepherd's Pie. 111
Shortbread Cookies. 167
Shredded Pastry Squares – Knafee 205
Shrimp in Tomato Sauce 124
Simple Fried Fish 122
Skillet Meat Pockets 144

Soups and Salads

Beef Broth 31
Beef Noodle Stew 35
Caesar Salad. 48
Chicken Broth 32
Chicken Noodle Soup 33
Cream of Broccoli Soup. 36
Egg Salad 46
Fattoush 47
French Onion Soup 41
Garden Salad 48
Greek Salad 43
Kishk Soup. 42
Lebanese Salad. 49
Lentil (Addas) Soup. 38
Lentil Soup with Beef 39
Lentil Soup with Lemon. 40
Macaroni Salad. 44
Minestrone Soup 37
No Mayo Coleslaw. 44
Potato and Egg Salad 46
Potato Salad 45
Tabouli 43
Taco Salad 50
Tomato and Cucumber Salad 50
Vegetable Soup. 34
Yogurt Cucumber Salad 45
Spaghetti 114
Spinach and Rice. 63
Spinach Dip. 19
Spinach Tortellini 67
Strawberry Vanilla Smoothie 26
Stuffed Baked Fish 121
Stuffed Grape Leaves – Warak Inaab 56
Stuffed Kibbi Balls 117
Stuffed Mushrooms. 17
Stuffed Zucchini – Koussa Mihshee 107
Sugar Cookies 167
Syrup 197

T

Tabouli 43
Tacos 104
Taco Salad 50
Tahini (Sesame Seed Paste) Cookies 211
Tangy Spinach Pies. 132
Taratur - Tahini (Sesame Seed) Sauce 13
The Ultimate Smoothie Milk Shake 26
Tomato and Cucumber Salad 50
Tomato Salsa. 20
Tortellini Alfredo 65
Traditional Rolls 156
Truffles 193
Tuna Melts 126
Tuna Wraps 128

U

Urban 146

V

Vegetable Soup 34
Vegetable Stuffed Pockets 145
Vegetable Tortellini 66

W

White Icing 183

Y

Yogurt Cucumber Salad 45
Yogurt Dip – Laban. 21

Z

Zaatar Pies. 138
Zucchini and Eggs. 64
Zucchini and Tomatoes 64